CW0554233

From Field and Fen

Mike Toms

Crow Meadow Press

From Field and Fen

ISBN 978-0-9933717-0-7

First Published in 2015 by Crow Meadow Press

Conceived, designed and produced by:
Crow Meadow Press
www.crowmeadow.co.uk

A catalogue record for this book is available from the British Library.

Set in 11/13.2 pt Adobe Garamond Pro
Printed and bound by CPI Group (UK) Lyd, Croydon, CR0 4YY

For Basil Patrick William Ernest Toms

Introduction

Places and landscapes change. Most of this change takes place too slowly for us to comprehend; a gradual, creeping alteration of our surroundings that seeps into our consciousness as the nagging doubts that haunt our memories. It is only when sudden, dramatic change occurs that we become alert; the jarring alterations to familiar landscapes perhaps sufficient to stimulate great sadness or raise an angry cry of loss.

We tolerate the changes to the landscapes within which we live because, more often than not, we do not see them; and we do not see them because we do not look. Landscape is a backdrop to our lives, a canvas that falls beyond the focus of our gaze. It is incidental, additional and over-familiar. Our focus has been shortened by technology, by the security of food and warmth, and by the increasingly urban-centred nature of our lives. It is only when we can spend significant periods of time with a landscape that we can begin to look properly and truly see the changes that are taking place within it.

This book is the result of looking, of spending a decade within a few small patches of landscape and of becoming attuned to the shifts and fluxes that would otherwise have been missed. It is a book about feeling and understanding that moves with the seasons and responds to the external pressures that are an inevitable consequence of the increasing demands on our land.

A consequence of spending so much time in these landscapes has been a shift in the way that I write about them. What began as simple descriptions of what was seen, and sometimes felt, has evolved to include a more moral narrative. The familiarity that I have developed with these scraps of landscape, from the scrubby corners of favourite fields to the twisted shapes of individual trees, has intensified my feelings. I no longer simply care about these landscapes in general terms; instead I care in particular terms. It is no longer the loss of a tree but the loss of a particular tree, one I have come to know as an individual, that pains me.

Attention to the detail of a landscape delivers increased appreciation and greater respect, something long commented upon by deep ecologists and those fortunate enough to have spent time within landscapes of such scale that detailed observation becomes a necessary mechanism for survival. Within my own, rather smaller landscape, I have become observant in more than one sense of the word. I have become alert to the landscape and its component parts but in a way that suggests some spiritual connection. My respect for this landscape requires an adherence to its rules – its cycles, processes and boundaries.

There is a good chance that you spend time within a landscape, or part of a landscape. No matter how small that patch, I would urge you to spend some of that time *with* the landscape and free from other distractions. Take the time to stand and watch, to immerse yourself within your surroundings. Just maybe, you may find some connection that will prompt you to look harder and see that landscape in a different way.

Acknowledgements

The pieces which feature in this book are drawn from a decade of articles produced for the Eastern Daily Press. To have been asked to contribute a regular column, and to follow in the footsteps of great naturalists like Ted Ellis, continues to be an honour and a pleasure.

This book would not have been possible without the support and generosity of the Eastern Daily Press and its staff, in particular my editors Trevor Heaton and Peter Kelley, and I am very grateful to them, and to Archant Community Media Limited, for allowing me to reproduce these articles in book form. I also owe a great deal of thanks to my wife, Lyn, who has proofread my articles ahead of submission, and to Liz Shaw for her work copy-editing the material as it as been drawn together in book form. I am profoundly grateful to Carry Akroyd, whose artwork graces the cover of this book and most likely prompted you to pick it up in the first place! Carry's own engagement with landscape can be seen through her many wonderful pieces and I am very grateful to her for supporting this project. There are many friends and family whose love and support have shaped the ways in which I see, engage with and respond to landscape; you all hold such an important place in my heart – thank you.

Spring

Such bright days as these, which are not spring
but hint so teasingly at her approach;
Such days that make my souful spirit sing
and rise, to look towards some finer thing.

Transition

It is the spring warmth on my skin that lifts my spirits, delivering the sense that winter has passed and that life is returning. Though changeable, these first few days of spring mean more to me than the warmer, predictable days of summer and I suspect that it is the feeling of renewal that sets this season apart.

The first small glimpses of this new beginning are equally reassuring: the splashes of colour as early flowers and shoots poke above ground. Amid the dull browns and dirty greys of the winter's leaf litter are dotted the crisp white of snowdrops and the bright yellow of winter aconite. Strictly speaking these are winter-flowering plants but, nevertheless, they point to the future flowerings that will herald the true arrival of spring.

The dawn air rings with the calls of rooks. Settled at their rookery, there is much society to be had as pairs reinforce bonds or bicker with their neighbours over the ownership of sticks destined for the nest. The clear skies and lack of foliage show the rookeries off at their best, the birds striking in their glossy black feathering and bone white faces.

While other birds are just beginning to sing or are still on their way back from African wintering grounds, the rook breeding season is well advanced. Most of these rooks will already be incubating a clutch of four or five eggs and it will not be long before there are hungry young in the nest. The blue-green eggs, with their pattern of speckles and blotches, were once the target of fearless children, willing to risk a perilous climb to steal an egg and demonstrate bravado.

It was the wildlife artist Eric Ennion who noted how spring came to Breckland via its river valleys, describing how the first flush of green reached these riverside habitats long before it touched the open warrens and heaths. Even now this pattern is repeated; flowering and bud burst are evident along the Thet and Little Ouse but the open heaths and clear-fell continue to be brushed with overnight frosts that leave the long-dead stems of last year's growth brittle and white.

As a strengthening sun warms the land, so you sense that spring is spreading out from the shelter of the river valleys to claim temporary hold on the surrounding land. The first brimstone; the first buzzing queen bumblebee and the growing chorus of bird song that shapes the transition from slumber to reawakening.

Spring's messenger

The bright yellow flowers of lesser celandine are one of the first woodland blooms of the year, their rich, golden yellow petals marking them out as members of the buttercup family. Lesser celandine is well distributed across Norfolk – and not just within woodland. It is a familiar plant in gardens, appearing in quantity around many Norfolk villages.

The plant occurs as two subspecies, each slightly different in habits and form. One, known as subspecies *ficaria*, occurs in more natural, less disturbed sites – notably areas of ancient woodland. The other, *bulbilifer*, prefers the disturbed ground that is found in gardens and other areas marked by human activity. *Bulbilifer* is a more aggressive plant, able to spread and form carpets of rich yellow and green in areas of heavy shade. Lesser celandine regularly throws up unusual colour forms, including those with white, pale yellow or even orange flowers. These do not persist, however, and are soon lost.

The timing of flowering has given rise to a now largely defunct local name of 'spring messenger' but it is for another local name that lesser celandine is better know. That name is 'pilewort', highlighting the herbal qualities attributed to the plant. The similarity of the tuberous root to the appearance of haemorrhoids led to celandine being used to treat piles, This principle, common in early medicine, held that if something in nature mimicked the appearance of an affliction, then it would serve as a cure.

Such primitive and potentially superstitious beliefs were exploited by commercial herbalists during the 17th and 18th centuries through the Doctrine of Signatures. The doctrine held that all plants carried some physical clue, formed by the Creator, as to their medicinal use. The leaves and roots of lesser celandine were crushed and then boiled in unsalted buttermilk which, once cooled, could be applied to the afflicted area.

Lesser celandine was Wordsworth's favourite flower, stimulating him to write three separate poems proclaiming its beauty. So strong was his association with this spring flower that, upon his death in 1850, its image was to be carved on his tomb. Unfortunately, the flower which appears on Wordsworth's monument at Grasmere is greater celandine. Despite its English name, greater celandine is not related to the poet's cherished flower; instead it belongs to the poppy family.

Waiting

I am standing on soft ground, a few metres back from a shallow drain that feeds into the main river just beyond this piece of wet woodland. Somewhere ahead of me, in the tangle of dead stems that surround the root plate of a fallen alder, is a water rail. The bird had been feeding in the open but ran for cover at my approach, underlining its secretive nature. Although I am hidden somewhat by another old tree, it also limits my view and the bird could already have moved away without me noticing.

I play this waiting game often, watching patiently in the hope that some bird or animal will re-emerge. At other times I select a likely spot with a good view and just wait to see what comes along. Not everyone has the patience to sit or stand still, often for the best part of an hour, but it is something that I have always done. I find that I am not so much waiting as gradually tuning myself into what is going on around me. I am garnering a sense of the place and, in some small way, becoming a part of it.

Take today for example; my ears start to pick up the gentle rustlings around me, the sounds of small mammals and birds working through the vegetation in search of food. I catch the soft calls of a tit flock as it moves through the wood, the shrill note of a treecreeper – probably in with the tit flock – and the distant 'chack' of jackdaws going about their business over the town. The more I listen, the more I hear.

There is a sudden 'pichou', the call of a marsh tit, and soon I have a pair of these birds working their way down through the canopy to my left. Lower and lower they descend until they reach the gurgling shallows of the drain, where they drink in turn, perched on an old reed stem. Wet woodland is a good place to find these birds which, because of their hole-nesting habits, require standing dead wood soft enough to take a nest hole.

A larger creature is now moving through the reeds and dead grass: a muntjac, most likely, because the woods are full of these stocky little deer. The river is no obstacle for them and on occasion one may be seen swimming from one bank to the other.

My attention shifts back to the spot where the water rail disappeared but there is no sign of the bird. I am a little pushed for time this morning and am forced to return to the path. As I step from behind the cover of the alder there is a flurry of brown wings as the water rail appears, taking flight and disappearing deeper into the wood. Today, it seems, my waiting was not enough.

Performance

Each evening I see them, even though the warming weather should prompt their departure. From a distance they appear as a smudge on the horizon, moving too rapidly and in too many different directions to be smoke from one of the chimneys. Passing up through town towards home I catch sight of them again. This time I am closer and the smudge dissipates to become a multitude of small black shapes, each one a starling performing its part in this grand aerial ballet.

On still evenings, as the sunlight begins to fade and is replaced by the artificial glow of the streetlights, the starlings come together in tight flocks that wheel about the sky. Waves of brown shadow pulse across the flock as birds turn in harmony; flexing like muscle, each bird responding in unison to some unknown instruction. All the while the flock is increasing in size as small parties of starlings come together, forming bigger groups that ultimately coalesce into a single fluid entity, numbering many thousands strong.

The presence of the starlings has not gone unnoticed and the local sparrowhawk can be seen most evenings, working the flock with characteristic poise. Selecting a single starling from the mass will not be easy; more often than not the sparrowhawk fails to secure a meal.

The performance lasts for an hour or more. Suddenly, as the last of the natural light slips away, the starlings fall like a shower of English arrows. Such is the speed of their descent into the thick cover, provided by a line of conifers, that a loud rushing sound is clearly audible. If these were arrows, then all that is missing is the dreadful sound of iron punching through armour and flesh. As the remainder of the flock wheels in ever-tightening arcs above the trees, so more and more birds flight down into their roost.

Later in the evening, as I slip out for a pint of milk, I pass the conifers. There is a soft babble of noise which reminds me of a concert audience just prior to the curtain lifting. The chatter has an edge of excitement to it; were one to anthropomorphise, you could just imagine the birds catching up on the day's gossip before settling down for the night ahead.

I wonder how long this urban roost will be tolerated. The sheer numbers of birds involved means that the cars parked at this end of the street are splattered with droppings, as must be the garden within which the conifers sit. Other roosts in town have been lost because of intolerance. Will this one suffer the same fate?

Our smallest carnivore

A narrow blur of warm brown flashes across the road ahead of me. Low to the ground, like a vole that has been elongated, this tiny, cylindrical mass of energy is a weasel. In an instant it is gone, a bounding leap taking it up onto the verge and out of sight.

This is typical of an encounter with our smallest carnivore; all to brief and wholly unsatisfactory. On those few occasions when I have come across a dead weasel, freshly killed by passing traffic, I have been surprised by its small size. Even the largest males only just reach 24cm in length and weigh less than 200g.

The weasel is found across most of England, Wales and Scotland but is missing from nearly all of our offshore islands. It does best where there are good numbers of its favoured small mammal prey (mice and voles) and is usually associated with the cover provided by hedgerows and old stone walls. Its small size, which opens it up to predation by larger animals, may be one reason why the weasel tends to avoid more open habitats.

At this time of the year the males are extending their exclusive territories, seeking access to potential mates by taking in the home ranges of a number of females. Individual weasels do not make their own dens but instead occupy those of other species (such as those of rats, mice and moles). The small body size is an adaptation, allowing the weasel to hunt and pursue small mammal prey into their runs and tunnel systems. This small size also enables it to raid nest boxes – predation of nesting blue and great tits increases in those years when small mammal numbers are low – underlining the weasel's agility above ground as well as below. In addition to birds, weasels may also take young rabbits, reptiles, amphibians and, on occasion, earthworms.

The weasel is a surprisingly pugnacious animal despite its small size. Over the years I have encountered a number of individuals, accidentally captured while using Longworth live-traps for project work on small mammals. The presence of a weasel in the trap is usually, but not always, revealed by a pungent odour and a sense of increased weight. The trap, which is traditionally opened into a large, clear plastic bag, may instead be opened onto the ground, allowing the weasel to escape. I can remember one particular individual very clearly; upon being released it turned and berated me for several minutes with a harsh chattering. What it lacked in size it made up for in character.

Feathering the nest

These early days of spring are some of the best of the year. There is a palpable sense of optimism, coupled with the promise of what lies ahead and a feeling that winter has passed. The weather of recent weeks has prompted a rising chorus of bird song and many species have already started their breeding attempts. From around town have come reports of blackbirds, collared doves and robins with eggs.

Today, however, my attentions are elsewhere as I try to establish where the long-tailed tits have made their intricate nests. We have a dozen or so pairs breeding on our local nature reserve and locating their nests for the British Trust for Ornithology's Nest Record Scheme has become a regular feature for the start of my nest monitoring year.

Long-tailed tit nests are some of the easiest nests to find but only if you can watch the adults back to the nest site. This is best done early in the season while each pair is still constructing its nest, which is made from moss, tied together with silk from spiders webs and then decorated with lichen. Once the domed structure is complete the birds line it with feathers, perhaps delivering as many as 2,000 feathers over the course of several days.

Following a long-tailed tit back to the nest is fairly easy if the bird happens to be carrying a feather in its bill.

It is not long until I catch up with a pair of birds doing just this; their presence first revealed by the calls that they appear to deliver almost continuously when in each other's company. The birds flick along the hedge-line and then cross the track to enter a long bramble bush within which they have nested in previous years.

Once the birds leave the bush, the feather having been deposited, I go and take a closer look. By squatting down low to the ground I can peer through the bush, which lacks the thicker growth of later in the year, and silhouette the nest against the sky. It is on the far side of the bush and I know from past experience that it will be a painful approach through other brambles to reach the nest for monitoring.

The long-tailed tits will continue to add material to the nest over the coming weeks, the rate of delivery much reduced, and I wonder if they leave the nest at this almost finished state in order to test whether it is hidden well enough. Carrying so many feathers to a nest might reveal its presence to a potential nest predator, so taking a pause before investing in eggs would seem a sensible strategy. For me, with the first nest of the season found, it is time to move on and search for others.

Breckland meres

I have long been fascinated by the Breckland meres, a series of 12 permanent waterbodies quite unlike anything else in England. Self-sustaining, their dramatically fluctuating water levels prevent the establishment of reedbed, swamp or, ultimately, woodland. With the exception of Mickle Mere, none have any visible inlet or outlet, the variations in water level resulting from the height of the water table within the surrounding chalk. When the water level is high, the meres may overflow; when it is low, they may dry up altogether.

During their dry phases the bare mud is soon colonised by some rather interesting plants, including the rare liverwort *Riccia cavernosa*. During the wet phases many of the meres support rare invertebrates, species characterised by their ability to survive long periods of dry conditions either by burrowing down into the damp soil or by surviving as a desiccated egg.

In centuries past, locals would have taken advantage of the dry conditions by planting root crops in the rich soil revealed by retreating waters. Sometimes the meres would remain dry for more than a year but water levels could rise suddenly and locals might lose their crops or be forced to finish harvesting in knee-deep water. These days the water levels in the meres are maintained through a management plan that controls the level of the water table by halting extraction for agricultural uses if there is a threat to the meres. The meres must be allowed to drain every few years, otherwise the delicate balance needed to retain their character and unique biological identity would be lost.

The Breckland meres are also fascinating because of the history associated with them. Excavations at Mickle Mere and West Mere have revealed the presence of prehistoric lake dwellings, suggesting a long period of human use of the sites. Ringmere was the site of a fierce battle between Danish invaders and the Saxon ruler Ulfkytel. The Norse scald (scribe) Ottar described the battle and noted how '*from Hringmar field the chime of war*' was heard. The battle also appears in the Anglo-Saxon Chronicle, where it is noted how the Saxon force, camped by the mere, was beaten through the treachery of a servant with Danish ancestry.

Looking at the meres today, it is only through the knowledge of these ancient writings that one can take away a sense of their permanency. It would be all too easy for the meres to be lost; another part of the landscape consigned to the pages of history.

Woodlarks abound

The sky is dark and brooding, almost autumnal in nature, and the strength of the wind makes me feel that I may have chanced my luck in coming out this morning. The weather forecast predicted that the overnight rain would have pushed through soon after first light and I am rather hoping that the scatter of raindrops on the car windscreen is the end, not the beginning, of a belt of showers.

The moody sky suits the open landscape of the Surrey heaths; the open vistas are spared the horizon-shortening banks of conifers that spoil so much of my native Breckland, hemming me in and compartmentalising the landscape. Many of the Surrey heathlands have been shaped by the military and have only recently been taken on as nature reserves. They remain open; a mixture of sandy soils sloping down to wetter ground, abundant pools and (in summer) a multitude of dragonflies and damp-loving plants.

The cloud and wind combine to deliver a chill and I am glad to be on the move, striding across the boardwalk towards the higher ground ahead. Despite the weather there are a few birds singing, the melancholy fluty whistle of curlew, the ever-present wren and a distant snatch of woodlark. It is the woodlarks that I have come to see, even though they are a familiar bird at home in Norfolk.

Here, on Thursley Common, they are doing well, with a good number of breeding territories spread across the ground that lies around me.

I can see that the bank of cloud is slipping away to the southeast and the brightening sky brings much-needed warmth, not only stirring my spirits but also prompting other birds to start singing. Finding some higher ground I stand in the sunshine and watch one of the woodlarks perched, as they so often do, in a suitable tree. Singing from a silver birch, one of many that seem to have lost their tops, the woodlark is beautifully lit in the spring sunshine and it fills the telescope's field of view. Smaller than a skylark, this species is noticeably short-tailed and has a strongly patterned head.

I'm soon watching other individuals, some singing and others foraging on the ground amongst the heather. The common was damaged by fire two summers ago and many of the trees remain blackened. Woodlark numbers have increased over recent years, no doubt contributing to the numbers on show this morning.

While I see them almost daily in Norfolk at this time of the year, I never see them in these numbers, nor in such striking surroundings. It was worth chancing my luck with the weather.

Rookery

This is rook country; a late Easter break has brought me to the undulating pasture-lands and woodlots of Dorset, where the green of spring is a week or more in advance of that in Norfolk. The still bare trees that crowd the narrow lanes are topped with the nests of rooks, upturned cones of sticks collected from nearby or stolen from the unguarded nests of neighbouring pairs. Many nests have rooks in attendance.

Dressed in funereal black, these are splendid birds; their ragged loose-winged forms rise effortlessly from the trees in the brisk wind, sweeping away to feed on the slowly warming turf. Others attend to unfortunate creatures that have been killed by traffic, scavenging much-needed protein from road-kill badgers and rabbits. A closer view in the strengthening sunshine reveals a plumage that is not simply black, but is instead dressed with a wonderful mix of bronze, blues and purples, reminiscent of the way in which oil on water separates out into a kaleidoscope of colours.

It is the social cohesion of the rookery that provides a real sense of the vitality of spring, more so than the sight of newborn lambs or a woodland alive with the calls of the first chiffchaffs. The sound of a rookery at dawn is something else, providing a bustling sense of the activity that is taking place within this vibrant community. Yet, most English rookeries contain fewer than 50 nests and only a handful have been recorded with more than 300. A few really big rookeries have been recorded in the past, notably on large Scottish estates. The trend, certainly within England, has been towards smaller rookeries, perhaps a reflection of food availability, loss of suitable nesting trees or increased levels of disturbance.

Levels of activity vary throughout the day and also change as the breeding season progresses. During the period of nest construction, raiding parties of young birds attempt to steal twigs from unguarded nests. For this reason, breeding females will usually guard the nest while their mate seeks out suitable twigs. Only when the lining of the nest begins is the female confident enough to join the male in collecting material.

Once the nest is complete the female begins to lay her eggs, producing a clutch of two to six eggs which she will then incubate alone over the coming weeks. As the season progresses, so the expanding leaf cover hides the rookery from prying eyes, halting our glimpse of the busy collective lifestyle of these birds.

A sight of sulphur

The first of the spring's butterflies is always a welcome sign; not the peacock disturbed from its winter slumbers in the woodpile or the small tortoiseshell that has spent the winter in the cool of the spare room but one that has truly emerged from hibernation, brought to life by the rising daytime temperatures. The other morning, venturing into the forest, I chanced upon my first butterfly of the year, a brightly coloured male brimstone, sulphurous yellow in colour, soon to be followed by others.

That these individuals are on the wing so early in the year stems from the fact that they have chosen to overwinter as adults, fattening up on autumn nectar before finding somewhere suitable to pass the winter months. For a brimstone the chosen site will often be deep within an evergreen shrub.

Just a handful of our butterflies overwinter as adults. Along with the brimstone, small tortoiseshell and peacock there are the comma, red admiral and large tortoiseshell, the latter now extinct as a resident. Other species pass the winter as caterpillars, eggs or as pupae, with each species overwintering at the same stage each year. There is an exception to this rule: the speckled wood spends the winter as either a caterpillar or a pupa, the stage dependent upon late summer temperatures.

The brimstone has the longest adult lifespan of any British butterfly. The individuals on the wing now may have emerged from their pupal stage early last July, and they may continue on the wing through into this June or even July. The brightly coloured males emerge from hibernation before the females and can be wide ranging in their habits. Over the coming weeks the males will meet and court the pale-coloured females, initiating what the great lepidopterist and illustrator F. W. Frohawk described so beautifully as '*a prolonged dalliance flight in the sunshine*'. The eggs will be laid towards the end of May, each one deposited singly on the underside of buckthorn or alder buckthorn leaves.

It is an encouraging sign to see so many on the wing and equally reassuring to hear of other reports from across the county charting the emergence of other species. This might suggest that the cold weather has had little impact on their overwintering success; a good omen for the coming season.

Shades of purple

The land is greening as increasing day length and warming temperatures stimulate new growth. In with the green are welcome splashes of colour, the first of the year's flowers providing early nectar for newly emerged insects. Alongside the shouty yellow of celandine are the softer purple tones of red dead-nettle and ground-ivy. I have always liked the soft purples of these small springtime flowers, perhaps because they are understated or perhaps because you have to get down on your hands and knees to really appreciate them.

Both red dead-nettle and ground-ivy are overlooked plants, often regarded as weeds within the garden by those who do not appreciate their aesthetic or wildlife value. This is a shame, not least because ground-ivy was once a well-regarded plant. Take a closer look at ground-ivy and you will see that it is a softly hairy plant, with blunt-tipped, kidney-shaped leaves, each of which is strongly toothed. The flowers are pale violet in colour (sometimes almost pink) with delicate purple spotting.

Ground-ivy sets very little seed but instead spreads vegetatively through the rapid growth of its creeping stems. This habit earned it the local name of 'blue runner', now no longer in use. Although it is common and widespread, the species appears to be increasing within woodland habitats, particularly in southern Britain. It is thought that this is a consequence of expanding deer populations, whose preferential grazing on more palatable herbs has favoured the bitter-tasting ground-ivy.

It is this bitter taste that has seen ground-ivy used in tonic herbal teas and, occasionally, in salads. The early Anglo-Saxons, who used it to clarify their beers, made greater use of the plant. Added to a brew, the plant improved flavour, extended the time over which a beer could be kept and also improved its clarity. The beer was referred to as 'gill-ale', derived from one of the English names for the plant; another name for the plant, associated with the brewing of beer, was 'ale-hoof'. The practice of using ground-ivy in this manner continued up until the reign of Henry VIII, at which time it was replaced in this role by the hop, a cultivar of which was introduced into Britain during the 16th century.

There were other local uses for the plant. In Shropshire it was used as a stuffing at Easter for a leg of pork and, elsewhere in Europe, the leaves were eaten by French peasants during autumn, when their flavour was further strengthened by the presence of brown galls formed by a small wasp.

Herald the queen

The sound of a queen bumblebee is a sure sign of spring. Newly emerged from winter hibernation, these large and fascinating insects will soon be searching for a suitable site in which to establish a nest. With their internal fat stores almost exhausted, the first priority is to seek out sources of early season nectar and pollen.

Although the buff-tailed bumblebee may be seen visiting the catkins of sallow or garden flowers as early as February, the other common species are rarely on the wing so early. It is a precarious time; early emergence may use up valuable resources if there is insufficient nectar and pollen to be found. If the weather turns cold then the bees will seek shelter and become torpid, re-emerging once the weather improves. By the beginning of April all the common species will be on the wing, engaged in finding food. Interspersed with these bouts of foraging are periods spent sunbathing on exposed leaves, walls or stones, a behaviour that is thought to help with the development of the ovaries in readiness for egg laying.

There is then a change in bumblebee behaviour, with the introduction of low, contour-hugging flights, as individuals prospect for a suitable nest site. Preferred nest sites vary with species; while some bumblebees nest underground others may use old bird nests, nest boxes or tree cavities. The underground nests tend to be in the abandoned burrows made by small mammals, like mice and voles. These can be a scarce resource and competition for nests may be fierce. It is sometimes possible to find several dead queen bumblebees around the entrance of a small mammal nest being used by a victorious queen.

The whole process of nest site location and selection may take several weeks but, once the nest is established, the queen soon gets on with the business of producing her first batch of eggs. Typically, the queen will line the nest with fine material, before constructing a brood chamber that is made of wax extruded from her abdomen. It is into this chamber that she will lay a batch of eggs, usually between eight and 12 in number – the queen having mated back in the autumn before going into hibernation. Alongside the brood chamber the queen will have constructed a nectar store. This initial batch of eggs will deliver the first infertile workers that will tend subsequent broods but the queen will need to tend this first brood herself.

Dinner is unfurled

The sap is rising and all around the countryside things are springing into leaf. Fresh green leaves, often miniature versions still to expand to their full size, see a welcome return of green hues to the landscape. The stark, two-dimensional forms of branches are now clothed and the dry soil beneath shaded by an expanding canopy of life. These new leaves will power this season's growth, enabling many trees and plants to lay down reserves that will see them through the distant winter.

This flush of green serves another purpose and is already being eyed by hungry bugs that will chomp, munch and slurp their way through its plump cells. The caterpillars of various moths will be some of the most numerous of these eager herbivores. While some will live on the surface, trimming back the fresh growth, others tunnel their way through the soft tissue leaving behind them characteristic 'leaf-mines' full of frass. Caterpillars are not the only creatures to mine the leaves; various sawflies, flies and beetles also make a living this way.

Some of these mines will be familiar enough. The horse chestnut leaf miner has made the headlines on numerous occasions since it first reached our shores. The sheer size of its population on individual trees can turn an entire canopy rusty brown and there have been calls that something should be done. It might well be that the population of this particular leaf miner settles down to a more respectable level over time, in much the same way as was the case with the firethorn leaf miner a few years ago.

The mines made by many of the small leaf mining moths tend to be all that we see of the moth itself, so small are they in size. These diminutive creatures, just a few millimetres in length, are some of the most beautifully patterned of our moths, adorned as they are in tufty golds, shining purples and wispy whites. Some of the other leaf feeders are equally impressive but many adopt more subtle tones, attempting to blend in with their surroundings to avoid the unwelcome attentions of would-be predators.

Nevertheless, the vast number of leaf-feeding invertebrates is a food resource that is fully exploited by nesting birds. Resident tits and newly arrived warblers will feast on this spring bounty, using it to fuel their own breeding attempts. So tightly are some of these birds tied to their invertebrate prey that their breeding success is dependent upon them matching the timing of the peak in their chicks' growth with the peak in caterpillar abundance. This, in turn, is linked to the timing of bud burst and that first flush of green.

Origami with leaves

Things have really started to green up over the last few days, the vibrant fresh greens of new growth adding new colour to a previously dull canvas. Look closely and you will see that there is a clear succession to much of this greening. Trees in particular provide an opportunity to spot which species come into leaf first. Over the last few days the garden rowan has come into leaf, while the hazel is only just bursting through from its buds. The buds on the beech, on the other hand, remain firmly sealed, the leaves inside yet to put in an appearance.

Many of the newly emerged leaves have quite a bit of growing still to do; look at those of horse chestnut for instance, miniature versions of their final form. In contrast, the beech leaves will emerge almost fully formed, raising the question of just how they can be packed into such a small bud.

It seems that the key to this trick lies in the way in which these new leaves are folded. Researchers have discovered that the angle between the midrib of the leaf and the lateral veins that emerge from it determines how the leaf will unfold. This angles varies between different tree species, ranging from 10 degrees to almost 90; the bigger the angle the more compactly a leaf can be folded and, hence, crammed into a smaller bud.

This space-saving option comes at a price, since the larger the angle the more slowly the leaf expands. Beech has an angle of roughly 40 degrees (ranging from 50 near the stalk to 30 near the tip), allowing it to expand to its full area that much more rapidly. This strategy lies behind the long leaf buds that you see on beech, each containing a virtually fully formed leaf, folded ready for deployment.

That we know all this is down to work carried out by a team of scientists working in Japan. They have spent time studying the mechanics of leaf emergence, even using paper to replicate the nature of the unfolding process. An understanding of the principles of leaf emergence and, in particular, how you cram a large flat object into a much smaller three-dimensional space, has value elsewhere in science by highlighting how we might overcome particular design problems.

This area of science is known as biomimetics and has been used to look to nature for solutions to design issues, from folding tents through to the deployment of solar panels on satellites and other spacecraft. The mechanics of nature are something from which we can all learn.

A narrow escape

The two Egyptian geese are watching something. Stood on the riverbank by the ancient crossing point they are alert, their heads focused on the river and their whole bodies rigid in posture. On the river itself is a female mallard, her mate in attendance close by, and both birds protectively close to an early brood of ducklings. While the chicks huddle together, the adults have adopted the same rigid, straight-necked posture as the geese. My immediate thought is 'otter' but it takes me a few moments to pick up the tell-tale trail of bubbles that reveals its underwater presence.

The otter surfaces close to the far bank, deep in the shadow of an overhanging willow, before the head slips back beneath the surface and the trail of bubbles begins again. This particular individual seems to be working the bank and can't yet have noticed the mallards and their vulnerable youngsters, exposed in the middle of the gentle flow. I too am now watching nervously, waiting to see if the trail of bubbles will move away from the bank and out towards the mallard family.

The otter emerges for air, this time exploring part of the riverbank in greater detail while on the surface. Surely it must have noticed the ducks just a few metres away? By now the otter is parallel with the ducks and this is the critical moment. Will it continue to work the bank or slip out into the current to take one of the ducklings? The next time the otter surfaces will provide the answer to this question that means life or death to one or more of the birds on the river.

The bubbles continue, close to the bank, and I feel my body relax as it becomes clear that the otter will not strike out towards the mallards. I watch as it continues to work the bank, all the time moving further upstream. The ducks, however, remain tense and the chicks hang in the current, almost motionless beside their parents.

Finally, after what seems an age, the birds relax and turn to ride the current downstream and away from the otter. As I continue on my way I replay the scene in my mind. How did the otter not see the mallards and their young? Perhaps more importantly, how did the ducks – not to mention the geese on the riverbank – spot the otter? Was it down to a chance glance across to the far bank, catching the otter at the surface?

Encounter with a spitting spider

As soon as I saw her I was pretty sure of her identity: *Scytodes thoracica*, the spitting spider. Once she was safely sealed in the confines of one of my specimen tubes I checked her identity against a guide and took in her spiderly beauty. Very pale brown in colour, *Scytodes* is delicately marked with a succession of spots on her thorax and strongly domed carapace, and bands on her thin legs.

The large, domed carapace is a striking feature and houses a pair of enormous double-lobed glands. Each front lobe produces poison while the larger rear lobes produce a sticky, glue-like substance. Each gland is linked by a duct to the front of the fang where it emerges through a small opening. By using muscular contractions to compress the gland, the spider is able to 'fire' a stream of poisonous glue at its intended victim, easily covering a distance of 10mm or more. At the same time, the spider very rapidly moves its fangs from side to side, creating a zig-zag of deadly spray that quickly immobilises its prey; only then does the spider approach more closely and deliver the *coup de grâce*. If there is any sign of a struggle on the part of the victim, *Scytodes* will deliver a bite to one of the extremities before retreating and playing her patient game.

As the weaponry might suggest, this is an active hunter which does not bother to build a web, but instead stalks prey with a slow and steady gait. *Scytodes* is synanthropic in habits, which means that she lives alongside us in our houses and offices. Although widely distributed within southern Britain, south of a line from the Humber to Glamorgan, this spider is either somewhat uncommon or poorly reported.

I have only seen the species on three occasions in the 15 years that I have lived in this old house and I do not recall seeing her in any of the other houses in which I have lived previously.

The spider's powers of dispersal may be rather poor; since its young do not disperse on the breeze, dispersal is likely to be through the movement of household objects from one location to another. Another factor that may restrict the species to low levels of abundance is the length of time (some three years) that it takes the females to reach maturity. We tend to think of insects, spiders and other invertebrates as being short-lived, ephemeral creatures but this is not always the case. Having secured her identity I release her, in the hope that she remains unnoticed by my wife!

Fishy business

It is good to be out on the water, sat in a large inflatable and at eye level with the dashing forms of early swallows and passing terns. We are here to ring nestling cormorants, a colony of which breeds in the trees that fringe Abberton Reservoir. There are five of us in all, split between the two boats which we paddle slowly around the reservoir, assessing the stage of each nest in turn before determining which to approach for ringing.

These inland breeding cormorants are part of an expanding inland population, a relatively recent development set against a longer history where virtually all of our cormorants were coastal in their habits. Part of the reason for this change has been the establishment of colonies of the continental race, known as *sinensis*. This race originates from breeding colonies in France and the Netherlands, where it breeds almost exclusively alongside inland freshwaters. Unlike our own race, *carbo*, the continental birds are migratory in habits and their arrival here has led to the establishment of these inland breeding colonies. The colony at Abberton started with just nine pairs in 1981, growing rapidly to a peak of 551 pairs in 1996, since when numbers have fallen somewhat.

Ringing cormorants is hard work. Not only do you have to paddle around the reservoir but you also have to spend a lot of time in the water, wading up to the partially submerged trees used for breeding, before erecting a ladder and climbing up to the nest. Then there are the birds themselves. Any adults in the tree, of which there are usually a few, retreat out onto the water to form a scattered raft of sleek black shapes with alert, periscope heads watching our activities.

The chicks are relaxed in the hand but invariably relieve themselves over you and, occasionally, bring up a lump of partially digested fish. It is smelly but important work. Each of the chicks receives both a standard metal ring and a special colour ring, the latter marked with three large digits that can be read at a distance using binoculars. These colour rings enable researchers to collect far more information on the movements of the birds than would otherwise be possible.

Our visit to each small cluster of nests is brief, just 10 or 15 minutes on a warm day like this, allowing the adults to return to feed their chicks with minimal disturbance on our part. I know that cormorants are not the most popular of birds with fishermen but there is something truly endearing when you encounter them as soft-feathered youngsters.

Swift

It takes a few moments for the soft, drawn-out screech to penetrate the layers of memory but then, instinctively, I tilt my head back and scan the sky for the source of the sound. The screech comes again, this time overlapped by a second, and my eyes pick out the crescent-shaped forms of two swifts against the deep grey of the passing shower clouds. They are back, these sentinels of summer; these all too brief visitors from south of the Equator are here and I feel a surge of overwhelming joy.

The return of the swifts draws out a stronger response from me than my first calling cuckoo, twittering swallow or scratching sedge warbler. Quite why this should be is impossible to explain. Being brought up in the countryside, I came to live alongside swifts rather later in life than I did these other returning summer visitors. Perhaps it is because I have spent the past decade living in an urban centre, where the swift is virtually the only summering migrant, that this bird has come to signify summer's arrival so much more strongly than any other.

Still watching the sky I pick out a third individual, the small party twisting and turning as they feed, before sweeping across the sky in long and shallow arcs. The swifts continue this display for many minutes and then drift off behind the rooftops of a neighbouring street.

Are these 'my' birds, the individuals that will breed in the roof-spaces of some of the houses along my street, or are they passing through, still on their journey north? Over the next few days I expect to see more individuals gathering in the sky above the garden and to hear that soft screech of summer.

I like to imagine the journey that these tiny birds have made, to picture the different landscapes over which they must have flown, and the upward glances of those people who share our swifts when they are elsewhere.

For a swift the passing of a year is all about the journey; ever on the move, swifts spend such a small part of their year here in England that we can hardly claim ownership over them. This is, however, the one place where they come down to 'touch' the Earth, where they settle briefly to breed, so perhaps our connection with these wonderful birds holds greater significance than for those over whose lands they are merely passing while on their great annual journey.

The supreme songster

In a scrubby thicket at the end of a fence line a sweet voice proclaims the presence of a nightingale. It has been some time since the reserve last held one of these migrant songsters and it is a delight to be able to take in the vibrant tones of his repertoire this close to home. The nightingale's song has a power and tonal range that is truly staggering. There have been times when I have been fortunate enough to be close enough to a singing nightingale to really appreciate that power; the rising and falling notes literally ringing in my ears. Although the phrases may vary, there is a sequence of notes in which the nightingale seems to be winding up towards the explosive flurry of song that follows. It is little wonder that this small and otherwise unassuming bird features so prominently in literature and the arts.

Despite the numbers of nightingales being reported, this is still a scarce summer visitor and one whose population has been in long-term decline. Of equal concern is the shrinking breeding range, with the bird now absent from many former haunts. One of the factors contributing to the decline may be the growing numbers of deer in our woodlands. The grazing pressure that comes from increased deer numbers reduces the amount of low scrubby cover that nightingales favour for nesting.

Being a migrant, there is also the distinct possibility that the population decline is being driven by what is happening to the species on its wintering grounds. Our nightingales almost certainly winter in West Africa, something that is supported by a small number of individuals fitted with tiny tracking devices by researchers. One bird, caught and tagged near Methwold Hythe on 25th July, was in northern France a week later, heading south and passing through Morocco in late August. By November it had reached Senegal, where it remained until February and the start of its journey north.

It is Norfolk's fenland edge that holds most of East Anglia's breeding nightingales, and the bird has been lost from many of its former haunts in the Brecks and along the scrubby margins of mid-Norfolk's river valleys. The presence of this local individual gives hope that things might be improving but we will have to wait to see if he secures a mate and attempts to breed. If he does, then his song should all but cease once the eggs hatch; if he keeps singing then it is likely that he remains alone.

The land of the rabbit

I often encounter rabbits when I am out and about in the Norfolk countryside. The dry, free-draining soils of the Brecks are well suited to their needs and it is no surprise that I see so many on my travels. There is a long history of this familiar mammal in the area and it would be fair to say that the rabbit has shaped the Breckland landscape and, at times, driven its economic fortunes.

Breckland was once a centre for the production of rabbits, with huge warrens maintained on many of the estates and an industry producing felt that continued through into the 1950s (and the arrival of myxomatosis). The rabbits were introduced soon after the Norman Conquest and the light soils of Breckland, although poor for crops, were ideally suited to these burrowing lagomorphs. Many of the warrens were operated by landowners but from the 15th century most were leased to professional warreners. Their legacy can be seen in some of the local place names and in the ruined lodges that once housed the warreners and the tools of their trade.

Many rabbits escaped from their warrens and damaged both crops and the landscape, altering vast tracts of land with their burrowing habits. The scale of the rabbit's impact can be seen in the writing of the time.

Gilpin had called Breckland '*the land of the rabbit*' and the fifth Earl of Albemarle, also writing in the 1800s, described the Breckland region as '*a mere rabbit warren*', noting that it still went by the name of '*the holely* [Holy] *land*'. Walk across a large and long-established warren today and you soon learn how difficult the going can be; with each step you run the risk of sinking a leg into a tunnel and turning an ankle.

Over time the rabbit industry faded, as farmers enlightened by new agricultural practices came to regard the rearing of rabbits as a wasteful and damaging practice. The rabbit continues to make a living in Breckland; sometimes it is cast as a villain, eating farmland crops, and sometimes as a useful tool for conservation, maintaining the short Breckland turf that favours rare insects and birds like the stone curlew.

One of the best places to sit and watch rabbits is the Norfolk Wildlife Trust reserve at East Wretham. Watching them can change your attitude towards them. To see their social interactions or watch their response to a passing stoat shifts them away from the image of a brown blur bolting for cover to a creature of interest and worthy of study. The rabbit will continue to play a role in our countryside for generations to come.

The lifeblood of the town

To imply that a river is the lifeblood of an urban landscape is an overused metaphor. Nevertheless, the way in which it pulls life into the heart of the town suggests that this is an appropriate acknowledgement of its pivotal role in shaping urban biodiversity. The river is a corridor, one along which creatures can move into the town, cutting through the barrier of suburban gardens, ring roads and fringing industrial units with their superstores and retail parks. Along much of its urban length it is corralled by concrete, its flow controlled by weirs, gates and pumps, but there are places where it retains a more natural character.

Thetford's lifeblood comes in the form of the Little Ouse and the Thet, both slipping silently in from the east through the old part of town and skirting what was once the town's economic heart. It is this first stretch that most often holds the interest of the local otters. From the Nuns' Bridges, which mark the ancient crossing point, it is possible to watch pike hang almost motionless in the current or the dark forms of chub that jostle in loose shoals. At this time of the year the surface dances with drake mackerel mayflies, the males swarming through until dusk, the lazy fish rising to gulp down those that tire and drop to the grasping surface film.

Despite the beauty of the river and its valuable role, we treat it badly. The combination of fine weather and a school holiday leave a myriad of coloured debris in the form of drinks cans, crisp packets and discarded clothing. From time to time the appearance of a bicycle, television set or CD player hints at the discarded trophy of a burglary, or the waste of someone too lazy to visit the recycling centre.

Perhaps the worst treatment is meted out through the subterranean pipes that drain into the river along its length. Some of these catch surface run-off from the roads, silently flushing salt and chemicals into the water, where they mix with nitrates from farmland and who knows what else.

More obvious than these invisible additions is the occasional discharge of oil, a black slick of which was seen entering the river just the other week. The quantity involved suggested that it was a deliberate act, the oil tipped into a drain that ultimately led to the river. It is incredibly frustrating that people seem to care so little, and that they remain oblivious to the damage they inflict on a living system that brings life to their town.

Summer

Haunter of the waterweed
You hang, in the current brooding.
Snarl of mouth that offers no escape
For rudd, roach or duckling.

The cuckoo's calling

I am not sure which is the more unpleasant: that I am stood in four feet of muddy water and have a leak in my chest waders, or that an unscheduled thunderstorm has soaked me to the skin and put an end to my reedbed nest monitoring for the evening. It is not even as if I get paid for this monitoring work! I am a volunteer, like dozens of others around the country who give up their time to monitor nests in support of conservation and research. What I do get, however, is the opportunity to see our birdlife from a privileged viewpoint, plus the knowledge that what I am doing is making a difference. And that, as the television adverts insist on telling you, is what life should be about.

That I am wet from top to toe does not matter; it has been a beautiful evening. A female cuckoo calling upon my arrival, various damselflies dancing just above the water's surface and the reedbed echoing to the chattering songs of reed warblers. So far, none of the dozen nests in this particular reedbed have been parasitised by the cuckoo, but many are yet to contain eggs and there's a good chance that the cuckoo will pick her moment and lay her deception into the nest of an unsuspecting pair. When she does, I will have the solemn task of completing two nest record cards: one charting the demise of the warblers' own nesting attempt (failed due to being parasitized) and one charting the fortunes of the single cuckoo now demanding the full attentions of its unwitting foster parents.

Anecdotal reports suggest that it has been a good year for the cuckoos, with many being reported from across the county. A fellow volunteer, monitoring a site not far up the road and just on the edge of the Brecks, has found 17 cuckoo eggs so far, the output of two different females working his site. Given that reed warbler numbers are on the increase and cuckoo numbers in decline, one hopes that we will see a few more successful cuckoos this year. The cuckoos do not have it all their own way, however, and the cuckoo chicks will have to face many challenges if they are to gain independence and successfully navigate the long migratory journey that lies ahead.

Dawn

Although it is not yet five in the morning, it has been light for over an hour. I would say that the morning is still and quiet, save for the chorus of singing birds, but there in the background is the low thumping beat of yet another illegal rave in the distant forest. I am becoming crepuscular in nature, feeling most at ease during the brief hours of dawn and dusk – that period when a certain calm descends over the natural world, as if the animals and birds themselves are unsure about the transition between day and night.

It is at dawn that many creatures seem more approachable and this is certainly the case this morning. Sitting exposed, towards the top of a dead dock, is a grasshopper warbler, reeling out its fly reel song. With head angled up above the horizontal the tiny bird proclaims its ownership of this patch of fen, slowly, almost mechanically, turning its head from side to side. It is a magical sight; later in the day the song will continue but by this time the warbler will have retreated into denser vegetation to remain hidden from view.

From across the fen come the dawn songs of other warblers: reed and sedge, with whitethroat chipping in. These birds, each holding their own small territory, are contributing to a cacophony of sound. To me, this chorus is the archetypal sound of spring, revealing how our fens, woodlands and hedgerows are alive with breeding birds.

Today there is a more exotic song, echoing out from the blocks of poplars that sit alongside the fen. Vaguely tropical in nature, it is the beautiful fluting call of a golden oriole, a scarce but annual breeding visitor. Several individuals have arrived since my last visit and I spend much of the next hour engaged in a game of hide and seek, searching out brief glimpses of the yellow and black males as they sing from high in the canopy.

Peering in from the track, between the rows of poplars, I am rewarded by all too brief views of several individuals and then, a little later, three in flight between adjacent woodlots. It is a magical time but even this early I do not have the place to myself. Such is the draw of these exotic visitors that others have risen to see them. Later in the day, many more birdwatchers will arrive, lining up along the banks to get their brief glimpses of the orioles. While they may go away happy with what they have seen, they will have missed so much – all those other birds that have greeted the dawn but are even now beginning to fall silent.

After rain

After rain the countryside becomes a different place, the air refreshed and deliciously scented with sweet earthy odours released from the now sodden ground. The muggy, heavy air is gone and with it has gone the lingering drowsiness that tends to creep over me on these warm and sultry days. The greens of the vegetation seem darker, as if the leaves and fronds have absorbed the moisture through osmosis to become plumped up and fleshy. Droplets of water form on the vegetation; coalescing under the influence of gravity into larger drops they slip from the leaves to fall noisily through the canopy.

The beech trees are striking, their narrow trunks stained darker grey by the rain and rising up to a green cathedral roof. The trunks look like stone pillars and the regimented nature of their planting, with neat rows forming a thin veneer between the road and the brooding conifer plantation beyond, only adds to the sense that I am within some wonderful piece of natural architecture. The closed canopy has so limited the growth of other plants that there is no field or shrub layer and my gaze through the plantation is unimpeded.

Leaving the boundaries of the wood I slip silently out onto one of the wide forest tracks and then follow the line of power cables through the cleared ride. The grass here is long and unmanaged and, when dry, alive with various bugs (including bishop's mitre, a fitting species to find so close to the cathedral-like beeches). The grass is joyously wet and I delight at the way it tugs at my trouser bottoms and wets my shins. I am a child again, ignoring parental chidings about not getting wet, running through the meadows of memory with a broad smile on my face.

I can hear the soft calls of a party of long-tailed tits and it is not long before they are all around me, working their way back up the trail I have just followed. This is a family party, with youngsters in tow. These small birds, all fluffy feathers and lollipop stick tail, are a delight to watch. Some of the youngsters have wet plumage and appear bedraggled, further adding to their endearing character. The rain was heavy so I assume they must have taken shelter somewhere, only now venturing forth to search for small insects dislodged by the rain.

The heat will return; the vegetation will dry and the air will become increasingly heavy with moisture. Dark clouds will form, the atmosphere increasingly charged, and I will become drowsy and wish for the inevitable storm to break. I can then look forward to that feeling of refreshment that comes after rain.

The ancient Briton

There are signs of activity in the wood, evidence that the local badgers are engaged in their nocturnal wanderings. In some parts of the wood well-worn paths can be seen, striking across a particularly steep bank or out towards the pasture where the badgers feed. Then there are the latrines, rough pits into which the badgers defecate and which have an important role in territorial demarcation.

Elsewhere in the wood there is other evidence of the badgers' activities. A robin's nest has been ripped from the low bank in which it was hidden, the footprints of the culprit identifying a badger as the predator involved. Ironically, perhaps, the ripped-out nest is lined with badger hair, the robin scavenging pieces of hair caught on a nearby fence under which the badgers pass out of the wood and into the fields beyond.

The badger has an interesting association with humans, in that pretty much all of us know what a badger looks like, but very few of us have seen a live badger and many of us live close to active badger setts yet remain completely unaware of their existence. The strong black and white face markings, the shuffling gait and the strong social ties within a group of badgers make the badger an engaging creature and it is easy to see why so many people have taken them to heart.

There is another side to our interactions with this most ancient of Britons; it is a darker side, which has seen the badger persecuted, baited and culled. Badgers were once persecuted because of their perceived impacts on game and fox hunting interests: the former because they opportunistically eat the young and eggs of ground-nesting birds and the latter because they supposedly compete with foxes for access to earths and setts. They are still baited with dogs in some areas, a vile and illegal practice that is thankfully becoming less common.

Then there is the issue of badgers and bovine TB, which has controversially resulted in a controlled cull. Regardless of the role that badgers may or may not play in the spread of bovine TB, and of the need to protect the livelihoods of farmers, it does seem morally wrong to target a species purely because it has some impact on our lives. After all, such impacts are minimal compared to those we are having on the countryside and the other creatures with which we share it.

Dusk

It is still light when we arrive, the brightness of a summer's day slowly slipping into the softer tones of evening. We are in the forest to catch and radio-tag nightjars for a student studying their ecology. Having chosen suitable spots, we quickly set our fine mesh nets and retire to a nearby forest ride to await the arrival of night and the stirring of the nightjars. There is time now for patient watching and hushed conversation.

The background drone of flies dissipates and the final birdsong slips towards silence, a solitary song thrush a last bastion of the daytime brigade. The time for the 'night watch' approaches and the first of the evening's bats appears: a noctule, an early riser that can sometimes be seen feeding alongside swifts, hawking the air for flying insects. The bat makes several passes up and down the ride and I curse myself for having left the bat detector at home; it would have been good to 'listen' to the noctule as well as watch it pass.

The colour begins to leach out of the vegetation as the daylight fades to replace greens and browns with silvers and greys. A short squeaking note, much like a child's toy, catches our attention and we glance up to see the dumpy form of a woodcock silhouetted overhead. The forest seems to support fair numbers of these rather unusual waders – a woodland rather than coastal bird that probes damp soil for earthworms and other invertebrates. Then we hear it, a soft mechanical churring call – a nightjar, distant but welcome. Soon it is joined by other birds, two close by and in the area of our nets – this bodes well. The closest of the birds is in flight, the churring interspersed with wing claps and calls, moving around off to our right. Then, it is silhouetted against the sky, its effortless, buoyant flight taking it in an arc around us and up into the top of a nearby oak. The bird, perched on its song-post, is advertising its presence to other nightjars.

These first excursions provide breathtaking views and we can stand and enjoy them, knowing that it will be another hour before we can turn on the tape lures that should attract the birds into our nets. Being nocturnal, the nightjar has excellent visual acuity and would be able to avoid the nets if we tried to operate them in this half-light. A sheet of cloud has formed and by 10.30 it is dark enough to try our luck. Each of us manning a single net, tape lure running, we crouch nearby watching and listening, hopeful that we might catch one of these truly amazing birds.

A croak in the woods

I have never heard a nightingale croak before! That such a renowned songster should utter an agitated amphibian-like croak comes as a surprise. It is something quite unexpected, something that has passed me by all these years; an overlooked oddity that highlights the gaps that remain in my experiences of our wildlife.

Oaken Wood is part of a much larger expanse of forest that spreads, lush and verdant, across the Surrey/Sussex borderlands. Owned by the Forestry Commission, the site is managed as a reserve by Butterfly Conservation for its rich butterfly fauna, which includes such notable species as purple emperor, white admiral and wood white. It is also ideal for nightingales, the thick regrowth providing the scrubby cover they favour for breeding.

According to Tony there are a dozen pairs here and, as we move through the wood, snatches of male song echo from the shadows. Restrained though they are, these short, measured flurries suggest that at any moment the songster will break into an even louder and more resonant tune. Despite the thick cover, Tony notes that most of the nests will be within a couple of metres of the narrow forest rides along which we are walking, something he had been taught as a boy by his father, an old boy bird ringer whom I had met some years ago.

A soft *hweet* call stops us in our tracks – an off-nest female calling to her mate. Settling down just on the edge of the thicker cover and allowing our eyes to adjust to the gloom we watch and listen to see if we can follow her back to the nest. Tony takes up a position further into the gloom, prompting the female to issue a frog-like croaking call, the call that is new to me.

This very precise alarm call means that we are close to the nest and that it contains either eggs that are close to hatching or chicks. Over the next hour, a patient game of watching ensues; every now and then I catch a glimpse of the female, silhouetted against a patch of sunlight striking down through the gloom from a gap in the canopy. She is carrying food, so now it is certain that the nest has chicks.

The patience pays off, the female returning again and again to the same patch of loose bramble cover, beneath which we find the nest, a surprisingly large affair with its deep cup and five dark chicks. In the soft, droning gloom of the wood it is a very intimate moment and I feel privileged to be here and to share the wood with these wonderful, croaking birds.

The river

There is something deeply soporific about the river. It moves with a nonchalant ease, the surface silky smooth and the presence of a current only betrayed by the steady underwater ripple of waterweed. Spared from the immediate effects of recent rain, the water is clear, the gravel bed visible for the first time in weeks. Such is the clarity of the water that the strengthening sun casts shadows within the water column itself; those cast by the waterweed dance and toy with the stones on the river bed.

The air above the river is crowded with tiny flies, each catching in the sun's rays which stream down from gaps in the overhanging trees. The trees themselves cast deep shadow, combining cool and heavy shade with the dry brightness of the sun and making it difficult for my eyes to adjust as I scan from one to the other. Here and there, patrolling dragonflies cruise in level flight before returning to a favoured perch to watch for rivals or pick out a passing female.

Standing on the bridge, one of my favourite viewpoints from which to watch the river and the life that surrounds it, I can see a shoal of small fish. They seem to favour the shallows, or is it that they are easier for me to spot there? I can make out the red of their fins, suggesting they are rudd or roach.

It has been a while since I have seen any larger fish in this stretch of the river. Perhaps they have been fished out or, more likely, they now favour one of the deeper stretches up-stream. There used to be a shoal of chub here that I would see virtually every day, but they, like the pike, are nowhere to be seen. Sadly, so close to the road, the river carries the scars of its human neighbours. An old mattress half covers the slowly rusting frame of a bike and other, smaller, items are scattered nearby.

Leaving the bridge and moving upstream, the taint of the river's human neighbours is lost and she regains her graceful elegance. The banks are thick with emergent growth and it is only because I am on higher ground that I can still see open water. Away from the traffic, the air carries a soft hum, the combined droning wing-beats of a myriad of insects. The pitch of this sound resonates within me and adds to the sense of somnambulance. It is a wonderful feeling to immerse myself in the life of the river in this way and I understand just why it is that I am drawn to her margins.

Evening

The air is warm but not quite still; here on the fen a male marsh harrier uses this to his advantage as he hangs momentarily above the edge of the reeds. It is a perfect summer evening, with the calm of dusk already beginning to descend upon the scene. A grasshopper warbler whirrs his reeling song, echoed a hundred times over by the softer extended buzzes of calling bush crickets. A few late dragonflies hawk for smaller prey, moving as if controlled by busy electric motors, driving them forward in a rapid mechanical motion.

And there, where the reedbed pushes up against the base of the poplar plantation, the dark grey scythe of a hobby drifts past with lazy ease, pitching upwards into a stall that sees it land in one of the trees. The hobby is perched below the reach of the setting sun, in shadow, but such is the strength and colour of the evening light that it remains beautifully lit; its rufous 'trousers' and black mask dress it as a smart toreador. Will I get to witness its *ballet de mort*, as it toys with the sweeping swifts feeding in ever-ascending arcs up into the fenland sky?

Out on the water are coot and grebe, all with young in attendance, while closer by a party of swans feeds and utters soft sounds of reassurance. Large carp break the surface of the river; their rotund bodies briefly make me think of porpoise, so glossy smooth do they appear in the changing light, with water clinging to them like some wet mucous skin. Along the bank and out into the flooded shallows wade the hefty forms of cattle, with calves in tow, all chewing their way through mouthfuls of luxuriant riverside vegetation. Perhaps disturbed by these bovine interlopers, a grey heron heaves itself up into the air with laboured wing-beats and moves off down the river to find a more peaceful fishing spot.

Smaller birds can be heard and fleetingly seen within the reedbeds that sit below the level of this bund. The bund guides me out and leads me along the sinuous edge of the river, past the great stands of poplars to the expanse of flooded reeds and open ground within which the two pairs of nesting cranes remain so well hidden.

The occasional call reveals the continued presence of the orioles, whose young successfully fledged from their high nests over the last two weeks. This is a special place to be on such an evening, highlighting in so many ways why an English summer can be so magical. I feel at one with the creatures around me and know that I have found my true place in this landscape.

Royal colour

On hot sunny days it feels as if high summer reigns throughout the Brecks. Areas of flowering grasses creep with the short buzzing calls of grasshoppers and the longer, high-pitched reels of bush crickets. Stands of deep green bracken and a backdrop of brooding conifers create flat blocks of colour against which the yellow-greens of dyer's rocket and the soft purples of viper's bugloss stand out as highlights on a wider canvas.

I have always liked the bugloss, providing, as it does, a richness of colour at a time when other plants are coming to the end of their flowering season. I like the tenacious way in which it brings life from the dry, sandy Breckland soils. It is a plant that does well here, the features that made it unpopular with arable farmers now helping it to eke out a living on this poor ground.

Vipers' bugloss is a member of the borage family, with roughly hairy stems that make the plant prickly to the touch and a deep taproot that makes it difficult to lift from the soil; no wonder the local farmers gave it the name 'devil's guts'. The plant was formerly a serious arable weed here, a reputation that it has carried with it to other countries, notably to Australia and New Zealand, where it has been introduced. Although I have seen it referred to as 'Paterson's curse' by an Australian, this local name should really be applied to the closely related purple viper's bugloss, a species introduced to Australia from the Mediterranean region.

The '*bugloss*' part of the plant's name has its roots in the Greek '*bous*' (an ox) and '*glossa*' (a tongue), a reference to the shape and rough texture of the leaves. '*Viper's* probably comes from the Roman physician and writer Dioscorides who knew the plant (or more likely knew its Mediterranean relative mentioned above) as '*echis*' (viper or snake). Dioscorides noted that the plant could be used as a treatment for a snake bite. This is a form of sympathetic medicine, where something that superficially resembles the cause of a problem can be used to treat it. In this case it is the seeds of viper's bugloss that resemble the heads of tiny snakes.

The dry forest soils on which the bugloss does best are also those on which I most often encounter our reptilian vipers, though I won't be putting my faith in the plant's seeds should I have the misfortune to be bitten.

Breaking the journey north

It is a short stop on a long journey north, made possible because the quarry at Bishop Middleham is just a four-minute drive from the A1. Stopping the car in a small lay-by, a half-hidden sign directs us through a gap in the hedge and into a belt of woodland. After 100 metres or so of walking through the damp, heavily shaded woodland cover I wonder if we have stopped in the wrong place. The map I had looked at before setting off suggested that the quarry butted right up against the road. However, with the path suddenly turning and dropping downhill, I am reassured, guessing that we are on the right track.

Sure enough we soon emerge into sunlight, entering an industrial amphitheatre that is carpeted with a short rich sward and surrounded by rising walls of magnesian limestone. Stone quarried from here was used for buildings, agriculture and various industrial processes. It is this history of quarrying that has shaped the community of plants and animals that thrives on these thin, magnesium-rich soils.

Large areas of the quarry floor are carpeted with the golden yellow blooms of common rock-rose and other lime-loving herbs, including eight different species of orchid. Among the pyramidal, bee and common spotted orchids are the tall flowering spikes of dark-red helleborine (an orchid by another name). This colony of helleborines is thought to number 2,000 or so flowering spikes, making this the largest colony in Britain. The plants are surprisingly tall and erect in habit, with thick and almost succulent leaves arranged in two rows up the stem. We are a little early in the season and the attractive dusky-red blooms are not yet open, the supporting flowering spikes hanging bent like the delicate curve of a shepherd's crook.

It is not the flowers that we have come to see, but a small butterfly – the northern brown argus. This species occurs from the Peak District northwards and is on the wing from June to August. The population at Bishop Middleham belongs to a distinct race, known as *salmacis* and first described in 1828. It is more commonly referred to as the Castle Eden argus, a reference to the part of County Durham where it is found. Although the weather is not ideal, with thick shower clouds rolling through and blocking the sun, our fortunate timing coincides with a sunny spell and we are rewarded by really excellent views of the butterfly and some photographs to take away. If we're passing this way again then another visit may well be in order, such is the richness of botany on display.

Bright lights

We are huddled around a moth trap on the southern margins of Thetford well after midnight, yet there is still the drone of traffic on the road to Bury. It has been a steady night so far, with a good mix of species in reasonable numbers, each drawn to the bright mercury vapour light of our moth traps. A low purr hints at the portable generator that provides us with the power needed for the traps, but it will only be when the fuel runs out that we will become aware of its intrusion into the still night. By that stage, dawn will not be far away and the passing traffic long ceased.

The strength of the light makes the darkness beyond all the more intense, our night vision gone. Moths buzz past our ears, occasionally blundering into us, pulled in by the light. You get a sense of the size of the moths as they approach, the more robust species trailing a whirr of heavy wings. With us are some people new to mothing and they are soon astounded by the colour and diversity of the moths on show. While the pink and ochre of an elephant hawkmoth creates a stir, it is the size of a pine hawkmoth that draws the most comment. This smart but rather neutrally toned species is a common catch in the Brecks at this time of the year. This is hardly surprising given the scale of the plantation forestry nearby.

The pine hawkmoth favours areas of open or mixed pine forest and is most strongly associated with the dry heaths and poor soils which have been devoted to timber production. It is the spread of these plantations that has really benefited the species. A century ago this moth would have been a rare vagrant here, but now Norfolk is well within its core range, a range that extends west into Dorset and north to Yorkshire. As its name suggests, the larvae of this impressive moth feed on pine trees, favouring the needles of Scots pine. When small, the larvae lie along the length of a needle, relying on this slender camouflage for protection. They grow in a rather sluggish manner, becoming more conspicuous before later descending to the ground where they overwinter as pupae under a carpet of moss or needles.

Adults are on the wing from May through into early August and are attracted both to light and to sweetly scented flowers. The females are initially reluctant to fly and remain on the trunks of trees where they await a male who will pair with them. The males, however, are more mobile and it is these that you tend to see in the traps. This is fortunate for us and for those who have joined us tonight for this moth trapping treat.

A scarce spectacle

Orchids, with their elegant blooms, have a reputation for being showy plants. There are, however, several species that rather let the side down and it was one of these that I encountered just the other weekend. In a damp and heavily shaded corner of a Suffolk wood I was shown 16 brittle-looking flowering stalks. These belonged to a small colony of bird's-nest orchid, a species more commonly encountered in the beech woods of southern England. To be honest the flowering stems looked liked long-dead plants but a closer inspection revealed that they were alive. Pale brown in colour, each of the individual flowers that made up the inflorescence was characteristically shaped. The sepals and petals formed an open hood at the top of the flower, while a double lip extended down below, the whole effect strongly reminiscent of common twayblade (a common orchid species).

The flowering spike represents the culmination of the plant's hard work, acquiring sufficient nutrient reserves below ground to produce and push up a stem. This process may take a decade of work, with the plant deriving these nutrients through a rather unusual association with a fungus. The bird's-nest orchid has virtually no chlorophyll and so is unable to carry out photosynthesis, the process so central to most plants.

Instead, the orchid gets its nutrients by devouring its living fungus partner which, in turn, obtains its carbohydrates through a symbiotic association with tree roots. In essence, the orchid has cut into a partnership between the tree and the fungus, exploiting both partners to its own advantage. The importance of the fungus is such that seeds produced by the orchid will only germinate where this particular fungus is present and this may be why these orchids are found in clumps within particular woodland patches.

The English name of the orchid is a reference to the appearance of the root system. Each plant has a rhizome around which a tangle of roots radiates out in an untidy manner. This looks very similar to the untidy stick nests built by pigeons and doves. The preference for damp ground within shaded woodland may be one of the reasons why this orchid has declined so dramatically across its historical range. There are just a handful of sites within East Anglia where this plant may be found and, particularly given the plant's appearance, it is probably best to visit a known site in the company of an experienced botanist rather than try to find one yourself.

The stillness of dawn

Even by my usual standards it is early; the combination of an elderly dog and a warm and stuffy night sees me up and about not long after four. Outside, in the garden, the air is delightfully cool and the town sits under a stillness that, for now, seems to suggest that its ownership rests with me. The dawn chorus of earlier in the year has subsided and it is the hypnotically drowsy calls of woodpigeons that echo across the dawn, disturbed only by the occasional chaffinch and dunnock.

The male from our resident pair of blackbirds stands in silhouette on the fence, a stroke of orange-yellow bill on an otherwise flat canvas. His plumage shows the signs of a long breeding season and the efforts of raising more than one brood of chicks. Scruffy in his appearance, it will not be long until the annual moult and the replacement of rough and battered feathers. The young from the latest breeding attempt are somewhere in the garden and they will soon start to call for food with the nagging persistence of hungry children – which, after all, is what they are. Other young birds will soon arrive. Streaky-plumaged young greenfinches in the company of their parents will come to take sunflower hearts from the hanging feeders and yellow-cheeked great tits will join them to take advantage of this reliable food source.

All of a sudden there is a brief moment of commotion as the jackdaws arrive. This gang of a dozen or so avian ruffians squabbles over scraps of food and tufts of discarded dog hair. For these birds the breeding season continues and there are hungry young to feed and nesting attempts to be completed. The jackdaws are always an early visitor, a pattern repeated in many other gardens across the county, and they only rarely visit the garden later in the day.

It is still a little too early for many insects to be on the wing, save the last of the night's moths. Once the sun makes her appearance and stirs the borders with her warmth, the bumblebees and hoverflies will emerge to jostle around the blooms. It is going to be another warm day but for now I can enjoy the cool stillness of dawn.

A dance of beauty

It is late afternoon and the muggy conditions cast a sultry feel. The shade on the river provides some comfort and I stand and watch the river from the stone bridge that marks an ancient crossing point. The water is running clear again after the rain of earlier in the week and the waterweed ripples in the slowly moving current. Towards the bank, where a shaft of sunlight cuts through the shadow cast by the bank-side trees, a school of small fish dance and glint just below the surface. I have seen pike here and these small fish face an ever-present threat.

A movement catches my eye, as from the shadows emerges the jewelled blue of a banded demoiselle, the county's most stunning damselfly. This species favours slow-moving rivers and the male is easily recognised by his wing band of brilliant blue. Only the male beautiful demoiselle is more stunning but, alas, the species does not occur this far east. The male banded demoiselle has a blue body, dark legs and robust, paddle-shaped wings.

This male is not alone; arcing out across the water he dances around another that has just appeared from under the bridge. The two protagonists circle each other, seemingly displaying at each other with a fluttering flight that is reminiscent of a butterfly. Even though there is no contact between them, I lose sight of which of the two was the original male. The dalliance over, one of the males loops back to the shadows from where the first emerged; this must be him, returning to his favoured spot.

It is only in our two demoiselles that damselfly courtship behaviour has been fully documented. The male responds to the presence of a female with a simple display in which he raises his abdomen and opens his wings. If she is receptive to these advances she will communicate this by alighting near him. He will then perform an aerial dance in front of her, first moving backwards and forwards and then from side to side. If the female remains receptive then he will approach and land, perching on her wing tips and then climbing slowly down onto her abdomen. It is then that he takes a grip on her to adopt the characteristic 'tandem position', something that you may well have observed in other damselflies.

These damselflies are a thing of beauty, so delicate that it is difficult to equate them with the squat larvae hauled from the silty root masses of waterside vegetation. The adults make a forlorn sight when you come across them on the nearby road, a life extinguished that should have been dancing jewel-like above the river.

The transition to evening

The swifts deliver stereo, a whole performance played out in the evening sky above me. Each scream, high-pitched with a rough and rasping edge, whizzes over and away at speed. The sound enters one ear, builds and then passes to the other like some carefully crafted accompaniment, best heard through headphones. Looking up from my book I see them, many more birds than the occasional drawn-out scream suggests; tiny, black bodies that scythe through the air on wings that beat rapidly and then solidify from blur to the solidity of a fixed-wing glide. Every now and then a group of these rapturous dogfighters wheels over in a low arc and I hear the rush of wind on their wings.

Five swifts blast onto my sky canvas from behind the towering height of the next-door semi; a sudden jolt of noise that makes me jump in my seat, so sudden is the appearance. As they bank they flash from black to silver like shoaling fish in a vast ocean that stretches away to the deepest blue.

Even here, not far from the centre of town, there is a stillness that descends with evening and with it the sense that the transition from day to night is approaching. The air feels heavy and moist, the dry drones of daytime insects replaced by the flutter and whirr of the first of the night's moths nectaring on the flowers around me.

Occasional noises from the back of the border suggest that larger creatures are also stirring, perhaps the wood mice that abuse my shed, raiding the bird feeders and amassing a winter store amid my carefully arranged clutter.

A nearer movement gives the sense of being more lumbering than the skittish movements made by mice and I watch its progress as the moving vegetation points to a likely emergence at the border's edge. Soon the source of the sound appears: a toad, replete and welcome. May he have a productive night feasting on the slugs that plague my tender flowers and vegetables.

By now my book lies face down on the table, the light faded to a point where reading is no longer possible. I pick up the sound of a feeding bat, the high-pitched echolocation calls still registering on my ageing ears. Every now and then I catch a glimpse of it as its silhouette flicks across the sky. It looks like one of the brown long-eared bats that catch yellow underwing moths and then carry them to the shelter of the passageway. There they will perch on the wall and remove the wings before munching noisily through the moth's succulent body. It is time for me to head inside and tackle the final chores of the day.

The old farm

It has been 25 years, probably more, since I last walked the footpath down the hill to Sturt Farm. Back then it was little more than a narrow, sunken track running across a series of fields, a crease in the sheep-grazed turf rather than anything more substantial. In the winter, when it snowed, we used to bring our sledges here and hurtle down a slope that steepened towards the bottom, accelerating you towards the barbed wire fence that marked the farm's western boundary.

The slope, the fence and the path are all still here but the path itself has changed dramatically. Another fence, presumably added to keep children on the path and out of the field, has allowed a tangle of vegetation to develop unchecked. Bramble, bindweed and bittersweet clamber over nettle and hawthorn, a new generation of ruffians exploiting the landowner's lack of interest in this small part of a once bigger plot.

The top of the biggest field has sprouted the beginnings of a wood, with clumps of hazel casting damp shade on this humid morning. The air under the trees resonates as if charged with static electricity, the whine of dozens of hoverflies all holding station. While the view from the path has been lost to the clambering plants, there is something deeply comforting about the tunnel of

green that the path has now become. The prying eyes of
the houses that push up against the farm's boundary can
no longer gaze on those few souls who use the path.

It is the silken nets of spiders, the lack of litter and
the way that the vegetation presses in that speak of a path
little used. Running down from the ridge, the path would
have once been well used, its sunken state testament
to the footfalls of generations past. Even though the
landscape has changed, the path seems rooted in the
history of this place. It is a link back through the years,
first to my childhood and then through the childhood of
my father to generations far beyond.

Two hundred homes are intended for this plot of
land, the planned access road to follow and replace this
ancient path. The landscape changes and we mourn
its passing but it remains resilient, secure in timescales
greater than we can comprehend.

Chalkhill blues

As I head southwest, out of East Anglia and onto
the A505, I leave the sandy Breckland soils behind and
cross onto the underlying chalk. Much of the chalk
grassland has been lost to agriculture and the remnants
are restricted to the steeper slopes of the chalk escarpment
and to areas of favourable land-use, such as horse racing
and golf. I am heading to the chalk grassland to search
out the chalkhill blue, a butterfly that is on the wing in
August at one of my nearest natural colonies.

Instead of stopping near Newmarket to view colonies
on the Devil's Dyke and Fleam Dyke, I am travelling
further afield to a colony on Therfield Heath, just to the
west of Royston. My reason for visiting this particular site
lies in its history. Therfield famously attracted butterfly
collectors from across Britain, each drawn by the lure of
the varied chalkhill blue colour forms found on the heath.
Most of our butterflies are known to exhibit unusual
colour forms from time to time, known as aberrations,
but the chalkhill blue is noted for having a greater range
of aberrations than any of our other species.

The population at Therfield Heath numbered many
thousands and early last century the heath would have
been inundated with collectors, each seeking that elusive
aberration to add to their collection. One particular

aberration, known as *semi-syngrapha*, in which the normally brown-coloured female has blue wings typical of the male, was the main target of the collectors.

The pressure of collecting, coupled with the cessation of sheep grazing, resulted in a dramatic decline in numbers and the population of chalkhill blues fell to dangerously low levels. These were restricted to the tiny pockets of suitable chalk grassland that remained, some only a few square metres in size. Fortunately, thanks to the efforts of local volunteers with an interest in the butterfly, the population was saved from extinction and since 1989 the number of chalkhill blues has increased.

One unusual aspect of the heath is the presence of a golf course, many fairways and greens of which are perched precipitously on the chalk escarpment. It is a large site and I thought that it might prove difficult to locate the discrete colonies. However, it does not take long to find the blues, the males actively quartering the vegetation in search of females that remain hidden below. These are delightful butterflies and seeing a dozen together makes me wonder how it must have been to witness hundreds on the wing when the population was at its peak.

Meadow

From the uncut meadow, where the purple-headed knaves of knapweed jostle with the flowering grasses, comes the song of summer's end. The buzzing reel of Roesel's bush crickets heralds the approaching shift in season and marks the slow transition from summer into autumn. That this small block of meadow is here at all probably owes as much to the economic downturn as it does to any 'green thinking' within the council's services department.

For many years this was a patch of manicured turf, the flowering plants suppressed by the mower's blades, but now it is thick with growth and bursting with life. As if to emphasise that this mini-meadow is still 'managed' the edge nearest the path has been maintained as lawn, a short sward that beats the boundaries of what is considered wild. It almost seems to serve as a warning – '*we can tame and subdue if we choose*'.

While it is here, and I fear it will not be long before it is cut, the meadow is home to many different insects; from the large and obvious meadow brown butterflies that rise and fall just above the sward, to the small and insignificant, like the froghoppers safe within their froth of cuckoo spit. Many hundreds of tiny spiders live within the sward, their webs picked out on damp mornings by the dew – a tented village of gossamer.

It is wonderful to see such a meadow so close to the centre of town, to see nature accessible and to hear the excited chatter of young children marvelling at the butterflies and bumblebees. Of course, the meadow is not untouched by the activities of other passers-by. Beer cans collect on the edge of the sward, where the short turf provides an opportunity for some to drink away their days; the council's litter bins, just feet away, are virtually ignored and stand mockingly empty.

The meadow is at its finest first thing in the morning, before the drinkers arrive. It is spared from their attentions because, to them, it is rough, unkempt and wild, its thistles and biting insects the custodians of this little patch of wild here in the centre of town. The meadow is not fenced, nor does it carry a notice board proclaiming its worth, but it does not need these things.

After the summer's heat

There is mist across the valley this morning, morphing the view into something less familiar and shortening my horizons. It is the first such mist for many months and hints at the approaching summer's end and a period of transition. The recent rain has replenished the parched ground and the air hangs heavy with moisture, as if the Earth itself has exhaled to release her sweet breath.

Walking the short turf of the lawn wets my feet and leaves behind footsteps that outline my passing, each a darker patch of moisture etched within the carpet of silvery white dew. Should I walk the meadow I would return with my trousers soaked, the fabric covered with grass seeds and the bodies of small invertebrates, each held tightly to the cloth by a meniscus of dew.

The air feels deliciously cool but carries with it the first sweet scents of autumn, the merest hint of woodland fungi that will undertake the process of breaking down much of the season's harvest. Two swifts pass overhead on silent wings, feeding as they journey south; they provide an echo of the noisy juveniles that were such a feature of July, just a few short weeks ago.

It is a morning that feels like summer's end, a shifting of the seasons and a sign that, to use a phrase from Ted Hughes, '*the globe's still working*'. This transition can be a gradual one, a lingering mix of days that sway between summer heat and autumn cool. There is a wish that summer will continue, that the warmth and light and life of summer will run on for many more weeks.

It is one of my favourite times of the year, with a strong sense that much of the natural world is on the move. Migrant birds from more northerly breeding grounds are already passing through on passage south. Many will attract the interest of birdwatchers, perhaps myself included, but for now I am content with my local 'patch' and the changes I can see within it, as the hedgerow fruits ripen, crickets chirp and house martins and swallows gather on the wires.

These cool mornings suggest renewal but of a different kind to that encountered in the spring, and my spirits soar as I experience the pull of season's end and look towards the approach of autumn.

Night on the river

Returning from the office late in the evening, I stop on the old stone bridge to scan the river. It is not quite dark and there is the possibility that I might spot one of the local otters. Tonight it seems I am out of luck and no dark shape appears, cutting its way across the surface of the slow-moving waterbody. Instead there are the dancing silhouettes of bats, hawking low above the water for insects. This small cloud of tiny, delicate mammals 'chatters' away with high-pitched calls as they circle to and fro to snatch midges and other small flies.

The chattering calls, whose intense high-pitched pulses I can still just about pick up with my hearing, are used to target prey through echolocation. This is really a highly developed form of sonar, the bat sending out short pulses of intense sound and then monitoring the returning echo with its sophisticated hearing to build up a 'map' of its surroundings.

Although many people are bewildered by the apparent complexity of bat echolocation, to the bat it is just another component of its sensory armoury – much like how we might view our sense of sight or taste. Bats make and hear sounds in the same way as most mammals; the echolocation pulses are generated in the larynx and the resulting echoes are picked up by the ears. Admittedly, the larynx of a bat is proportionally bigger than our own, relative to body size, because the call has to carry a great deal of energy in order to produce a useful echo. Most bats emit the echolocation call through their mouth but there are species, like the horseshoe bats, where the sound is emitted through the nose.

Because the echolocation calls of bats often differ in their core frequency, it is possible to identify the different species by the pattern of the call and the frequencies over which it occurs. For example, the calls of Daubenton's bat start at about 85kHz and drop to about 32kHz, with a peak in intensity around 45kHz. Simple bat detectors, which convert the inaudible calls to a frequency we can hear, can help you split bats into rough groups but more complex detectors, coupled with computer software, are needed to separate the calls of species which are similar in their outputs.

The size and behaviour of the bats hawking over the river suggests that these are one of our pipistrelle species, although there may well be a Daubenton's bat or two in with them. Perhaps tomorrow night I will have to bring a bat detector down to the river to find out.

A shift

There has been a noticeable chill in the air over recent mornings, the overnight drop in temperature sufficient to cast a heavy dew. The tall vegetation that flanks the forest rides hangs with seed-heads bowed by the weight of the dew upon them and tiny droplets of water glisten in the first of the sun's rays. The gossamer of a thousand spiders is draped over the vegetation like the silken threads of an untidy seamstress. Here and there a whole web, radiating out to points of firm anchorage, is stretched and contorted, pulled down by the weight of dew that coats its every thread.

Autumn is upon us. The screaming parties of swifts have left, deserting the rows of terraced housing, and increasing numbers of house martins are beginning to drift southward. The woods hold a scent of fungi, their fruiting bodies erupting through the surface to fling their tiny spores onto the strengthening winds. Reports of sandpipers and whimbrel herald the arrival of the first autumn passage migrants; with breeding finished they are free to move south.

I welcome this slow change, the steady transition between seasons, as nature turns through another part of her annual cycle. The lush, verdant growth of early summer is being replaced by mature browns as plants begin to shift their resources, either drawing back within themselves to fuel the spurt of growth that will come next year, or packing seeds that will soon be dispersed by a procession of unwitting accomplices.

This process of renewal fascinates me. I like the idea of drawing back within myself as the months of light and warmth pass, hoarding those experiences gathered throughout spring and summer in readiness for the winter ahead. By doing so I hope to remain in touch with the ebb and flow of the seasons, accepting the pattern of the natural world around me and not being blinkered by the narrow view offered by a world in which we can divorce ourselves from the seasons through artificial lights and gas-fired central heating.

This is why these first crisp mornings of autumn are so invigorating. My senses are alert to the changes in temperature and light, to the scents and behaviour of plants and animals, and I feel closer to the world around me. In some subtle way we are all influenced by the changing of the seasons. Perhaps we should acknowledge this more resolutely and celebrate these periods of transition, as one season passes into another.

Autumn

Under the bloodshot gaze of a harvest moon
the old witch hare crouches, her eyes ablaze.
Tight against the shadow of a field
caressed by the ploughshare's curving blades.

Greenshank

A scatter of showers has been passing through all
morning, some skirting the surrounding hills but others
rolling overhead to deliver waves of heavy, slanting rain.
With each approaching shower the wind lifts, white tufts
are created on the now rippling water and wading birds
are buffeted as they halt their southward journeys to
feed from the gleaming mud. I am in Rutland and this
particular lagoon provides one of the few opportunities in
the county for passing waders to stop over and feed.

Tucked, as I am, into the corner of a distant hide
I have only occasional company. There is none of the
blokey banter than can plague birdwatching trips to
more popular sites, with the endless ramblings of those
keen to tell you what they have seen at other sites and
in other countries. I can enjoy the birds alone, selfishly
undisturbed. Out front, hirundines rake the air, while
terns drop to pluck food from the water's surface and
dunlin and snipe haunt the margins. Two Egyptian geese
look wildly out of place, perched on one of the osprey
nest platforms, but perhaps this scene is closer to that of
their African homeland than it is to the ornamental lakes
and stately home backdrops of their adopted country.

A brief, ringing call alerts me to the presence of a
greenshank. Scanning with my binoculars I catch sight

of the bird as it flies in to land just 20 metres distant, the spear-tip of white that extends from the rump up the back bright against the darkening sky. The bird moves across the mud, tottering on exaggerated legs and with head facing into the wind. Every now and then it tacks left or right, head still down and forward, buffeted but never unbalanced.

The greenshank is a passage visitor to Rutland, perhaps from breeding grounds in northern Britain or, more likely, from further afield. This is a species of lonely uplands and forested marshes, a bird that moves south from late summer onwards, wintering in southern Britain, continental Europe and on into Africa. Most of those passing through eastern England will have begun their journey in Scandinavia and be heading for West Africa. The earliest of the birds to be on the move will have been underway in late July but passage will continue into November, making this a protracted period of autumn migration. I am sure that I will catch up with more of these elegant birds as the year tips towards its end but for now this individual has my full attention. It is a wonderful bird, understated and quietly elegant.

Crickets

There is a stillness to the morning, a calm that has draped itself over the river, delivering an almost soporific quality to the air. The river flows with a gentle ease, reflecting the lack of rain over recent days, murmuring its way quietly downstream. Only the steady chirps of dark bush crickets break the silence. These calls, with their resonant quality, have a tropical feel to them, suggestive of cicadas. Every bush or piece of waterside vegetation seems to host several crickets. Each one is sat squarely like a little toad, squat in posture and dark brown in colouration. The chirping call is an advertisement, directed at a potential mate.

I have come down through the meadows to collect two crayfish traps, set the previous evening. As I move through the vegetation I can smell the umbellifers and that strange aroma that I have come to associate with wet meadows. It is an almost acrid scent, slightly unpleasant and vaguely reminiscent of a public lavatory, but with an underlying sweetness. I remember how the short-tailed voles that I used to live-trap as part of a study into their ecology also had this scent and how it clung to my clothes after early morning rounds of my traps. Did the voles acquire the scent through their diet or because they lived within the pungent vegetation? I am sure a botanist could tell me its source and the chemical behind it.

The two traps are packed with crayfish, despite being in the water for only a dozen hours, and it is clear that this section of the river still supports a very large population of signal crayfish. An introduced species, this crayfish has wrecked river banks, reduced fish populations and eliminated our own native crayfish from most of its former haunts. Although I am trapping these signal crayfish in order to monitor their numbers, and to test the effectiveness of different types of trap, I am not allowed to release them back into the river. Instead, they must be killed and so end up in a pot, cooked and then served with a garlic mayonnaise.

As I trudge back to the car with my bucket of crayfish, I become aware of another cricket calling. This is Roesel's bush cricket, a large species with a distinctive high-pitched call. It sounds like a softly running fishing reel, of the old-fashioned style used for fly-fishing, and is one of the first sounds to disappear through the hearing loss that comes with age. I am glad that it is still part of my morning soundscape.

The garden by night

At night the garden becomes a very different place, the darkness shortening local horizons and the shadows shifting shapes and forms into unfamiliar contortions. Despite the darkness, I never find the garden or its shadows threatening. Instead it feels comforting, especially so on the last few warm nights of this Indian summer, when a low cover of cloud deepens the shadows and softens the nocturnal sounds of this urban area.

The garden feels more private, less exposed, and I am free to wander with my torch, searching out the army of small creatures that emerge with the setting of the sun. Dark brown spiders, almost black and somewhat flattened in their appearance, appear on the fence panels and the shed. They come in a range of sizes and it is interesting to see how they have divided up the vertical surfaces between them – the larger individuals well spaced, the smaller immatures less so. Examined more closely, their eyes burn bright in the beam of the torch and the subtleties of their colouration become clear.

Large slugs, mottled in appearance, leave trails of glistening slime across the patio that can be traced back to the shelters where they have spent the daylight hours, unmolested by birds. Then there are the snails, also moving about the garden on trails of slime. Many of these have spent the day under the lip of the wall, seemingly not as secure from predators judging by the number of smashed shells left by the hard-working song thrush.

Moths buzz the light of the torch, while others can be seen working the last of the season's flowers in the cottage garden-inspired beds. Some of these moths are immigrants, such as the silver-Y's which have appeared in smaller numbers this year. Others are resident, many of which feature frequently in my moth trap, tucked up against the wall to shade the neighbours. On warmer nights the number of moths in the trap is truly amazing, as is their variety of forms. Large stocky underwings sit alongside setaceous Hebrew characters, garden carpets and delicate thorns, beauties and pugs.

Elsewhere in the garden there is a speckled bush cricket. I cannot see it, since its call is too high-pitched for my ageing ears, but my bat detector picks up and amplifies the sound. The soft chirp of the male is intermittent but the detector suggests that it is sitting in the apple tree that overhangs the garden. From here it is calling for a mate, one of the few noises to break the nocturnal stillness.

A place on your table?

The combination of warmth and rain has triggered a mass of fungal fruiting bodies to emerge across the countryside. Fairy rings dot the grassland swards locally and little groups of toadstools adorn decaying stumps or cluster around the root balls of still living trees. Some of these fruiting bodies would make a tasty meal but knowing which requires a degree of skill and understanding.

Over the years I have sampled a number of different fungi; from the meaty textured cep through to the delicate flesh of the parasol mushroom and the butter-greedy giant puffball. My real interest is in the natural history of these organisms rather than their culinary value. Why, for example, are some species highly poisonous while others (even closely related ones) are edible (and rather tasty)?

One of our most dangerous species, the death cap, contains a cocktail of poisons that not only interferes with some of our body's most fundamental processes but also actively targets cell nuclei in the liver and kidneys. Death comes after a week and the species is responsible for 93% of all fungi-related poisonings in Europe. Despite this, slugs, maggots and rabbits all seemingly eat this toadstool with impunity. Is it a chance of chemistry that has made the death cap so deadly to us?

The death cap belongs to a wider group of fungi known as the *Amanita* and this group (of which we have roughly 30 species) contains toadstools with some wonderful names. Along with the familiar fly agaric, there are the panther, the blusher, the destroying angel and the aptly named fool's mushroom. While some are edible (for example, Caesar's mushroom – which has been prized since Roman times), most are inedible and a few deadly.

Several species are considered edible after thorough cooking. The toxins of the blusher, which attack red blood cells and cause a form of anaemia, are broken down by parboiling. The same is true of the toxins contained in the grisette and tawny grisette, two species that were formally thought of as being edible without the need for cooking! The *Amanita* are fairly easy to identify as a distinct group because they share a number of common features that can be seen in the field.

Separation of certain species within the group is, however, less easy. This is another reason why the comments made by one famous mycologist in describing these toadstools are best followed. He noted that this is a group of fungi '*to which it is better to devote a purely botanical interest than to give them a place on your table*'.

Gathering

This afternoon the heath echoes with the calls of stone curlews, several dozen individuals of which have gathered to lounge about and generally pester the local rabbit population. To my mind, this is the best time of year to watch them; away from the breeding grounds they are less sensitive to disturbance and they are more active, flying low overhead and interacting with each other. One other benefit of watching them at this time of the year is the lack of any heat haze, a common problem during the summer months when you are trying to pick the birds out from the bare arable ground on which they are sat.

Thanks to the efforts of local landowners, managing their land in a sensitive manner, the stone curlew population has undergone something of a resurgence in the Brecks over recent years. Following a low point in the early 1980s, when fewer than 90 pairs nested, the population had topped 200 pairs by 2007. Breckland has always been the heart of the stone curlew population. Stephenson – writing in the late 1800s – noted that '*... its presence in summer will enliven the waste for many generations to come*'. Of course, much of the 'waste' has gone, and the birds now nest on the arable land which has replaced much of the heath and sheepwalk that once dominated these Breckland wilds.

The stone curlew is predominantly a summer visitor, arriving on its breeding grounds from the middle of March. Interestingly, a few individuals have remained late into the winter at sites like Gooderstone and Hilborough. More typically, however, they depart for wintering grounds in southern France, Spain and North Africa during October. Prior to this (and typically from late July) the birds gather on traditional roosting sites, with newly independent young loafing about alongside moulting adults. Come evening, the birds disperse to other sites to feed. This makes late afternoon a good time to visit, the birds being more active than earlier in the day, and with more chance of seeing them in flight as well as on the ground.

It is a privilege to see these birds so close, and in such numbers. There is something of the prehistoric about them, most probably due to their huge bright yellow eyes and angular lines, and I could watch them for hours as they irritate the rabbits for no obvious reason or fly up at a rook that has strayed too close. But as daylight starts to ebb and the birds get ready to disperse, I know that it is time for me to head home and to leave my stone curlew watching for another afternoon.

The last round

There is a chill in the air this morning as we arrive in the pre-dawn gloom. The pits feel strangely still, a sign perhaps that this Indian summer has finally reached its end. We are here, among the reedbeds and lagoons, to set our nets for birds on the last of the season's netting sessions. Every ten days or so throughout the summer we have set our nets in fixed locations, with the aim of catching and ringing warblers, tits and finches as part of a wider project. All over Europe there are volunteers doing what we are doing: catching and ringing birds for science and conservation.

The nets are made of a lightweight material, the mesh sufficiently loose and dark that you soon lose sight of the nets against the vegetation. Strung throughout each net are horizontal threads, which produce 'shelves' within its length. A small bird, flying into the net, drops into the pocket formed by the shelf and is held gently until we extract it for ringing. It may seem a bit undignified but it does no harm and provides important information on bird movements, longevity and survival rates.

It takes nearly an hour to set all of the nets and, just before light, we go round them again to open up for catching. Already there is some activity, though little in comparison with earlier in the season when the site was packed with breeding birds. The soft calls of reed bunting and pied wagtail can be heard from one of the reedbeds. These are roosting birds that have come together to spend the night in the relative safety of the reedbeds. With a chill in the air we check the nets every 15 minutes, removing the birds we have caught and placing each in its own cotton bag.

Once back at the cars, where we have set up our ringing station, we process each bird in turn. Each is identified and then the appropriate ring for that species is selected and fitted. The rings are made of a soft, lightweight metal alloy and each carries a unique number and the address of the British Museum. If the bird is caught again, or found somewhere else, then we will know its history. We examine the plumage to work out its age (most birds moult in a predictable way that enables us to differentiate between old and new feathers) and its sex, before assessing weight and body condition. All done, the bird is released. Ringing provides a unique opportunity to see birds in the hand, to really appreciate their form and structure, and I feel very privileged to contribute to our understanding in this way.

In search of the wild

A recent taster for a new television series about the 'wild' has set me thinking about how little wilderness remains, not just here within our crowded island but more widely across the globe. With the advances in travel and technology there are few, if any, places that we cannot reach. In turn this means that there are few places that have not, in some way, been touched by our activities. Remote coastlines, unvisited by people, are still the recipients of our waste, in the form of plastic and other refuse that has drifted ashore from the sea. Inland valleys, inaccessible except from the air, may have been contaminated by chemicals carried in the rain, a residue of industrial pollutants now spread across the globe.

Our relationship with wilderness is important; it defines who we are and provides a measure against which we can judge our place in the world. One of the most important components of wilderness is the sense of scale, particularly given that so many of us now live within urbanised environments. The urban environment, with its narrow streets and ever-taller buildings, has removed the opportunity for people to experience (as novelist Wallace Stegner described) *'a sense of bigness outside themselves'*.

There is another, somewhat different, side to the wilderness that has long fascinated me; this is the sense of the wilderness (or the 'wild') as some dark and menacing place outside of our control. If you look at literature you will often see the wild described as a dark forest or a wood, within which strange and terrifying creatures exist. The association between the 'wild' and the 'wood' echoes down through the ages from a time when our ancestors first began to clear our ancient woodlands. Both 'wild' and 'wood' are thought to have developed from the same root word '*wald*', and the Teutonic word '*walthus*' (forest) entered Old English as '*weald*', '*wold*' or '*wald*'. These words were used to denote both a 'wooded place' and a 'wild place', cementing our association between the wild and the wildwood, as used by Oliver Rackham.

It is easy to dismiss the wild, the tracts of land that lie outside of our direct influence, and to think of them as waste; land that could be brought under the plough to meet our ever growing demands for food and materials. Yet the wild has a place, not just for the vast number of other species it supports but also for our own wellbeing. We should use the wild to question our sense of being, to test our perception of self-importance against the bigger world outside of ourselves.

Autumn morning

The edge of the wood is bathed in sunshine and I can feel the warmth of the sun's rays on my face as I emerge from the shadow. At the same time there is just enough of a chill in the breeze to underline that this is autumn, not summer, the strength of the sun's warmth diminished as we tilt away from her reach. The breeze also carries with it the sweet smell of a bonfire, seemingly out of sight behind the shoulder of land that separates this little valley from the larger one beyond. It is a fine morning to be out, enjoying the clarity of light that autumn always delivers.

It is too early in the day for the local buzzards to be abroad but other birds are much in evidence. A jay – I think it is just the one individual – is transporting acorns across the valley, preparing stores for the weeks ahead. Up to nine acorns may be carried during a single flight, the bird having a specially enlarged oesophagus and a liberal supply of saliva, both of which aid transportation. Autumn acorns are also taken by woodpigeons and rooks, so it pays the jay to hide those it can find away from the prying eyes of others. The jay's store will be tapped throughout the winter, often beginning within a few days of the wider acorn crop being exhausted. The degree of spatial memory required to find the buried acorns seems remarkable, and well beyond our own.

Turning south, I skirt the edge of the wood before tacking left down the slope to the gate at the bottom of the field. My arrival at the gate sends a scatter of rabbits to their burrows and prompts the noisy flight of a pheasant that had been tucked in close by. With the smell of the bonfire still lingering in my nostrils I can just about pick up the scent of a fox, perhaps an individual that passed this point overnight or just as the dawn was breaking. I wonder if it had been stalking voles in the thick grass that dominates this piece of rough pasture. Deer slots show that the fox was not the only large mammal to have passed this way. One or more roe deer have worked this edge since yesterday's heavy rain.

The hedgerow still has plenty of green colour, strewn with the dew-sodden webs of many hundreds of spiders and echoing to the wistful notes of a robin. A distant tractor hints that this is a working landscape and that I don't have it all to myself. It is time to head for home.

Radial architecture

It is on these damp mornings that the architectural skills of our many and varied spider species can be best appreciated. While bits of wall display simple webs, the gaps between plants support the more skilled constructions of orb-web spiders belonging to the genus *Araneus*. The most familiar of these is the garden orb-web spider *Araneus diadematus*, delicately marked with greys and browns and with a white cross on her back. It was the cross on her back that saw this spider venerated during the Middle Ages.

Dew-covered webs provide an opportunity to view the web's construction, revealing the fine threads formed by the spider during the previous night. The garden orb-web produces a sizeable web, with a defined central hub of meshed thread. Outside of this there is a narrow spiral, known as the strengthening spiral, which circles six or seven times around the hub. Radiating out from the centre are two or three dozen threads which stretch out to the stout outer frame. It is to these radiating threads that the main spiral is attached, the spiral beginning a little way out from the central hub. This leaves a gap, known as the free zone, between the strengthening spiral and the main body of the web itself. The main spiral is the key to securing a meal, since its threads are studded with blobs of glue. Flying insects unfortunate enough to encounter the web are held fast, affording the spider the opportunity to seize the prey and deliver a venomous bite. Some prey are deemed too large or too dangerous to be tackled and the spider simply cuts them free rather than risk injury.

Sometimes the spider will sit motionless, head down in the centre of her web, her eight legs alert to the vibrations caused by an insect caught in the web. At other times she will tuck herself away on the edge of the web and use a signal thread, which runs from her hiding place to the centre of her sticky trap, to detect prey. That the spider can move across the web with impunity, not becoming caught in her own sticky trap, comes down to her use of the non-sticky radial threads when moving about the web. She also has oily secretions, which cover her legs and reduce the chances of her becoming stuck.

These webs are particularly important to the female orb-web spiders, as they need to secure food in order to complete their series of moults and produce the eggs that will be deposited nearby at the appropriate time.

Lagoon

The sun is somewhat against us this morning; low in the sky, its strengthening rays silhouette the birds that are feeding or roosting on this large coastal lagoon. Even so, it is a pleasure to be out and to feel the late warmth cut through the thinning mist. Over the coming hours the sun will continue on its journey and the waders and gulls should prove less challenging to identify.

Close in, just a few metres from where we are stood, a small party of dunlin feeds in the shallows. In with them are a couple of curlew sandpipers, more elegant and refined than their dumpy counterparts. A water rail squeals from the reeds and, not long after, puts in the briefest of appearances. Full of character, and bubbling with personality, this is a bird to brighten up a morning's birdwatching. A few ducks are drifting across the deeper parts of the lagoon, a mix of teal, wigeon and shoveler, while many more doze, heads tucked in, on the small islets that poke above the silken surface.

A change of position and we are better placed to tackle the straggling flock of waders and gulls that extends part way across the lagoon. A dozen avocet are easily spotted among the large number of godwits, both black-tailed and bar-tailed; while some snooze, others stretch and preen. Scattered in with these leggy birds are a few smaller waders – mostly knot but with at least one ringed plover present. Behind these a run of spotted redshanks is revealed; about time, as we have been hearing their calls for much of the morning without seeing these smart birds.

A flock of golden plover arrives, providing a nice comparison with the grey plover – many still in breeding plumage – scattered on one of the quieter parts of the lagoon. Further away, where the forms of feeding birds are still difficult to resolve in the light, three spoonbills stand in the shallows. Newly established as a breeding species locally, these exotic-looking colonists are now a familiar sight here on the north Norfolk coast. It is a wonderful scene and one worthy of such an early start to the day.

Making a splash

Rain this heavy seems out of keeping with the season, catching me unexpectedly as I make my way home. A dry towel and a change of clothes, quickly followed by a warming mug of tea, soon restore lost inner warmth. As I drink my tea I watch the rain continue to fall. From the kitchen window I can see the heavy drops splash onto the surface of the patio, which dances under the deluge.

It is then that I spot the first frog, sat with its head slightly raised amidst the downpour. It soon becomes clear that this frog is not alone and that there are others on the patio, with yet more emerging from under the shed or from in between the flowerpots. Can there really be this many frogs using this small part of the garden?

I am interested that the rain should have tempted them out. I have seen the occasional frog on damp summer evenings but they have not seemed that common in the garden this year. That they should be here in such numbers takes me aback but it does remind me that there is plenty of food here to support them – the garden is on chalk and overrun with slugs and snails – even though it is in the centre of town.

The common frog is one of the few amphibian or reptile species to penetrate our larger conurbations. There is, however, good evidence that much of this penetration has been achieved with outside assistance. The fondness that we have for sharing frogspawn with friends and relatives may explain how frogs have been able to cross the 'concrete jungle' to colonise newly created ponds.

While the ponds are the focus for breeding activity, for much of the rest of the year these urban frogs will be living a terrestrial existence, largely out of sight. During the day they hide up in sheltered corners, under sheds and between flowerpots and piles of timber, before emerging at night as the humidity increases. It seems that a sudden rainstorm and an associated drop in temperature may bring them out earlier, much as it does the molluscs and earthworms upon which they feed.

Solitude

It is a damp afternoon and the light is not that good, but at least the rain has ceased and I have an opportunity to slip out of the house for an hour or so. I've come to the paddocks, an area I know well and where I can lose myself in patient watching. Setting up the scope I stand with my back to the ash and conifers, from which rotund drops of water descend noisily through the foliage. The sound of these falling drops is, for the most part, regular and soon filters itself from my hearing. Every now and then, however, a whole series of drops are set loose by one of the many squirrels that these woods hold.

Slowly I begin to unravel the soundscape: the soft calls of coal tits and goldcrests, a robin already in winter song and the distant calls of jackdaw off towards the house. Patience is the key here and I must stand quietly watching and listening. It feels much later in the afternoon than it actually is, the dark clouds adding hours to my perception of the time.

It is almost as if the creatures around me are settling down for the day, taking in a last feed before going off to roost. After a while the cloud thins and the light improves. As if prompted by this signal, a party of tits flutters through the hawthorns before crossing the track directly above my head. These are not the only creatures using the scraggy bushes in the middle of the paddock. A lone grey squirrel is picking hawthorn berries and, although partly hidden from sight, I'd say it was removing the pulp to get at the stones within.

Other birds are passing overhead: a steady stream of woodpigeons, a couple of jays, a small party of siskins and two cormorants, the last of these possibly on their way to the pits at Cranwich. Goshawk is occasionally seen passing over here but it is sparrowhawks that I see today.

There is much to be said for just standing and watching. It teaches you patience, as you slowly immerse yourself in what is happening around you. At times you can become possessive of the solitude that this form of wildlife watching delivers, frustrated should someone else stumble into your seclusion with a cheery hello and a questioning 'much about?'

On a damp afternoon like today I am left to the companionship of my own solitude and am able to spend a good two hours uninterrupted by nothing more than a distant tractor and a couple of low 'whumps' from the army range. I've had a good breath of air, freed my mind of any troubles and now feel in need of home and supper.

A new sound

There is a new sound in the half-light of early morning, a deep intonation that carries well across the otherwise silent forest. This is the roar of a red deer stag, one of at least three on my local patch who are taking part in a seasonal proclamation of ownership of a harem of females. Although typically described as a roar this challenge to other stags recalls the deep bellow of a bull. Unlike their upland cousins these sylvan red deer usually utter a single resonant groan, with long intervals in between each bellow. It is an unsettling sound in the half-light of dawn, an echo of a time when the woods of Britain were truly wild, inhabited by a range of large mammals now extinct.

The seasonal cycle of sexual activity in red deer is primarily driven by changes in photoperiod (the daily pattern of light and darkness) but it can also be influenced by the condition of the stag. Rutting is a draining experience and a stag may lose up to a fifth of his body weight, predominantly because of his greatly reduced intake of food during this period.

Beginning in late September, the rut is initiated by the largest and oldest stags who seek out traditional sites. Male red deer tend not to hold harems of females until they reach five or six years of age but they may find it easier to establish a harem in woodland than on the more open uplands of Britain, where red deer densities can be much greater than here in East Anglia.

As with many other animals, the act of attracting a mate has become a highly ritualised process. During the rut a stag will not only roar but will also thrash the vegetation, wallow and adorn himself with his own urine. In high density populations, individuals of comparable rank and size may end up fighting. After a roaring contest, the closely matched males may walk side by side, each presenting his bulk to his opponent. Then one individual will lower and turn his antlers, interlocking them with those of his rival. A pushing and twisting contest then follows which not uncommonly results in serious injury or even death.

The prize in all this display and aggression is access to one or more females and the opportunity to secure parentage of the next generation. While woodland red deer tend to have small harems, with seven or eight hinds in attendance, those on the open uplands will hold more. The rut will continue for several weeks, ending sometime in November. Until then, my morning walks will be blessed by this new soundscape, the roaring of stags.

The first geese

The first of the winter's geese are here and the morning sky echoes with their calls, as long skeins move between overnight roosts and daytime feeding grounds. These are pink-footed geese, newly arrived from Iceland and eastern Greenland, and their numbers will continue to grow over the coming weeks. Virtually the whole of the Icelandic and Greenland breeding populations winter in the UK, some 250,000 or so birds representing at least 85% of the world population. The only other breeding population is found on Svalbard, the individuals from there wintering in Belgium and the Netherlands.

These pink-footed geese will have arrived in Scotland several weeks ago, their arrival there continuing through into the middle of October, before most filter south to favoured sites. The bulk of the population winters in Lancashire or East Anglia, with Norfolk an important county for this winter visitor.

The geese are attracted by the combination of undisturbed roosting sites and daytime feeding areas. Initially, the geese wintered and fed on saltmarsh, feeding on grasses and herbs on the short saltmarsh sward. More recently the birds have taken advantage of the food available on areas of arable land and pasture, with sugar beet tops and waste potatoes a favoured food. Such choice does bring a small amount of conflict with landowners if the geese move from the harvested beet fields to feed on growing crops elsewhere. This happens more when the geese suffer high levels of disturbance, so landowners often grow the sugar beet away from footpaths and busy roads; this benefits both the landowner and the geese, which may go some way to explaining why the population has increased over recent years.

To me, it is the movement of pink-feet between roosting and feeding sites that is the most evocative part of the Norfolk winter. To hear an approaching flight of geese, which first appear as a distant smudge on the skyline but turn into distinct skeins as they approach, is truly magical. Equally magical is the sight of a huge flock, many hundreds strong, feeding across one of the larger coastal fields. To scan across these with a pair of binoculars reveals an army of individuals all feeding on the waste tops of beet.

In some ways it is a shame that they are only here for part of the year but I suppose that if they were here all year round then their magical charm would become commonplace.

A long life

I was raised within the sylvan embrace of the Low Weald, a well-wooded strip of country that rests on an ancient geology, now exposed with the eroding away of its covering chalk dome. To grow up among trees has left its mark on me and I always feel more comfortable in their presence, shaded and protected.

Trees have become an almost unseen backdrop to our lives. Their size and longevity, coupled with the fact that they remain rooted to one spot, seemingly makes them inconspicuous to casual observers. This also means that we tend to treat them badly, using them as architectural features – hemmed in by roads and pavements, or cut back indiscriminately because they block our view or shed leaves where we do not want them.

It is also fair to say that we do not, by and large, understand trees or fully comprehend our impact upon their lives. We have this conception that trees mature, become full of decay and, by doing so, reach the end of their lives. However, decay is part of the normal development of a tree and many trees will undergo retrenchment, reducing the area over which new wood has to be laid down by shedding branches and twigs, before going on for many more decades. While trees lack both an immune system and a wound repair system, they can wall off and bypass damaged tissue, effectively allowing them to redirect growth in a new direction and to balance this against incoming resources. This whole idea that trees have a defined lifespan and die of old age is something of a myth, for most trees are felled before they even reach middle age.

How long a particular tree has left to live, our intervention excluded, has little to do with how old it is but far more to do with its size and rate of growth. The truly veteran trees of Europe are not the oaks of landscaped parkland with their spread of great branches; instead they are the small twisted forms of cypresses, growing slowly on the high slopes of Cretan mountains. For trees that have in some way been managed by humans, it is those that have been pollarded which tend towards longer life. In both cases, it is adversity which has prolonged life, by slowing the rate of growth. Since so much of a tree's fortune will depend upon our influence, it is we who determine how they live and when they will die. Oliver Rackham, the great woodland ecologist, summed this up just perfectly when he noted that when it comes to life expectancy in trees the 'battlefield' is a better analogy than the 'almshouse'.

A sense of scale

There are parts of the Norfolk landscape that feel remote and isolated from the workings of humankind; stretches of coast where a bleak solitude can be found amid the dull tones of saltmarsh and the grand winter skyscapes. It is at this time of the year that these stretches of coast offer up their charm, the last of the holidaymakers now tucked up at home and only the hardiest of souls tempted out on a day when the bitter winds drive in off the sea. It is a good time to be out and about, to take stock of the summer's achievements and to reflect on seasons past.

Here, in Norfolk, it is the limitless horizon of the North Sea that delivers the special sense of place. By stretching away to meet the sky, it removes the sense of scale that seems ever-present elsewhere within the county. This landscape 'on the edge' moves me in the same way that I am moved by the great granite hills of northern Britain, the bleak moors of the west and the ancient chalk escarpments of the southern downlands. These are old landscapes and to be within them, part of them, reaffirms our place in the land.

The coastal saltmarshes, which echo to the haunting calls of redshank and curlew, are a fragile habitat, sensitive to changing sea levels and increasingly squeezed between the sea and prized arable land. Within Norfolk, however, the expanse of saltmarsh, which starts in the west at Thornham and stretches east as far as Cley, is largely protected from the direct impact of the sea by extensive shingle ridges and sand dunes. In recent years the defensive sea wall has been allowed to breach in places, part of a process of managed retreat.

The power of the sea is something that remains very difficult to deflect. Over the centuries the coastal fringe of Norfolk has been subjected to inundation, with periodic storm surges (or 'rages' as the Victorians called them) dumping huge quantities of seawater onto fresh and grazing marshes, changing the shape of the coast and impacting upon the lives of those who make their living there. It is a reminder that we do not exert complete control over the world around us, that there are natural processes that will shape the way in which we live.

Being here, at this boundary between land and sea, shedding the sense of scale, underlines the fact that we are part of a wider world. It removes us from the comfort of our day-to-day lives, something that it is difficult to do in our increasingly busy world.

Reedlings

Dropping down from the ridge running west from Burnham Market you get a wonderful view over Titchwell Marsh. On a bright November Sunday, you can see dozens of birdwatchers making their way to the hides that overlook the scrapes on Titchwell reserve. At this time of year there are many different birds to be seen from these hides and, with lots of eyes scanning the flocks of waders and wildfowl, there is always the chance of something rare or interesting. But today I want to avoid the bustle of the crowds and find some solitude worthy of such a clear day. For me, one place to do this is at Gypsy Lane. Situated to the east of Titchwell, a small lay-by marks the entrance to a narrow lane running north to the coast and passing through a succession of habitats.

The first part of the track is bordered by a strip of linear woodland, with a range of bushes and shrubs, from which the soft call-notes of foraging birds can be heard. It is well worth pausing to watch and listen as mixed feeding flocks, often of tits and late warblers, work their way past in search of insects and seeds. On this occasion there is no hoped-for rarity, like a Pallas's warbler, but there are goldcrests in with the tits. As the trees thin, there is a glimpse of two jays, another bird that, like the goldcrest, is much in evidence this autumn.

There are also glimpses out across Titchwell Marsh, over which hunting harriers may sometimes be seen – though not today. Then it is out from the cover of the woodland and onto the bank that puts you above the reeds, pools and saltmarshes which flank either side.

Almost immediately I can hear the scolding call of a wren from low down in the vegetation just a few metres away. Further off, I can hear the ringing calls of a small party of bearded tits as they move excitedly through the tops of the reeds. These are one of the birds I have come to see. Standing by my scope, I wait and listen as they move closer, slight movements in the reeds giving away their location. Finally they show themselves – brightly coloured and almost comical in appearance, these delightful little birds are always a joy to watch. Although they are scarce (nationally there are about 500 pairs), the counties of Norfolk, Suffolk and Essex hold about 40% of the breeding population.

Only part way through my walk, and with the prospect of more birds to see, the journey up to the coast has already proved worthwhile.

Stench

It is not so much the stench that gets you but the waste, the sheer volume of household detritus that is scattered layers deep over such a vast area. This is my first time on a waste tip and it is truly shocking to see the fragments of furniture, unwanted toys, endless plastic trays and countless shoes that have ended up here for landfill. This is not a place I want to be but it is where we stand the best chance of catching gulls for a colour-ringing project with which we are involved.

Setting the net is a well-drilled exercise; we roll out the hessian, onto which the net is neatly folded, then set up the 'cannons' whose projectiles, when fired, will carry the net over the feeding birds. Everything is checked and double-checked before we retreat some distance to wait. One of the bulldozer drivers adds some fresh refuse to the catching area and then the gulls appear.

Hundreds of gulls that had been loafing around the site take to the air and I am reminded of sleet against a dark November sky, such is their number. The first birds down to feed are the black-headed gulls, but the larger gulls quickly follow them: mostly herring and lesser black-backed gulls, with the odd great black-backed lurking menacingly. The net can only be fired when the safety-zone is clear of gulls so we miss taking several catches because of gulls standing too close to the folded net. The flock feeds quickly and then is gone. More fresh refuse is added and the process repeated until, finally, we can fire. There is a loud bang and the net is up and over the birds in an instant. We rush from our hiding place to secure the net and carefully extract the gulls, which are then placed in hessian sacks to keep them still and calm.

It is only when you get these birds in the hand that you appreciate the delicate nature of the black-headed gulls and the brute strength of the herring gulls. All of the larger gulls are immatures, either born this year or last, and we work our way through the sacks, fitting metal rings and recording biometrics before the colour rings are fitted. These also carry a number and are visible enough for birdwatchers to read the number from a distance and to report it.

The colour rings should tell us a lot about gull movements, something already evident from this morning's catch as we have caught a bird ringed in Denmark and one from the Czech Republic. One of the gulls, its foot covered in the expandable foam used by builders, highlights the hidden dangers of feeding at landfill sites and underlines our impact on the natural world and its other inhabitants.

November river

The river has become a different beast over recent weeks, the water levels higher than they have been for many months and the greens of summer growth now edged with brown, as water plants retrench ahead of the approaching winter. The riverside path has become slippery with fallen leaves; those from the many limes, paper thin in character, have been transformed into a delicate layer of yellows and translucent greens. Upon this are scattered the more robust leaves of willow.

The air itself is damp and heavy with scent. The earthy smells of fruiting fungi rouse the nostrils and hint at decay. Nature is busy, breaking down the growth of summer and secreting it away in a largely unseen cycle of renewal. It seems to have been a good year for fungi and an abundance of fruiting bodies adorns the stumps of trees, cut down in case they fall unplanned at a later time. Not everyone has appreciated the fungi; several of the path-side clumps carry the impression of a boot or shoe, too big to be that of an overenthusiastic child.

Elsewhere, other less obvious fungi can be seen. Small fruiting bodies emerge from the leaf litter or grow on the litter itself. Some adorn the trunks of trees, a dozen or more feet off the ground and safely out of reach of ignorant boots.

While it might feel as if nature is winding down, it is clear that there is plenty going on, even here where the river winds nonchalantly through the town. Shrubs and bushes are still festooned with berries and the trees heavy with seed. Returning blackbirds and migrant thrushes have plenty to feed on this autumn, so it is little wonder that garden feeders have been so quiet.

The changing of the clocks, coupled with the shortening hours of daylight, have restricted my riverside walks. While I am forced to take a less pleasant route to and from work, I know that life along the river will continue and that it will still be there, renewed come spring, when lengthening days once again open up the regular riverside walk and its wild creatures.

Soundscape

Writing in the 1920s, soon after the Great War and the loss of her husband, Helen Thomas recalled a trip that they had made together to the Wiltshire downs. From her description of the cottage in which they stayed and the natural world around it, it is clear that this experience of the countryside made a very great impression on Helen. One particular passage resonates with me and provides perhaps the best description of the silence that the countryside delivers. Helen wrote *'No other sound was to be heard, no trams, no people, no traffic, nothing but the sounds that do not spoil silence, but rather deepen it ...'*

For me, such words capture the true strength of the countryside and its stillness. It is not a silent world but one in which natural sounds enhance the sense of peace and welcome comfort. Helen's husband-to-be, accompanying her on this first trip, was Edward Thomas, a poet, reviewer and writer on nature and the countryside. Edward was a great walker. Prone to bouts of deep melancholy, he would sometimes stride from the house angry and bitter to seek relief through long hours spent alone, pacing through the countryside. Edward Thomas found peace in nature, the welcoming stillness of the countryside allowing him to battle his inner demons and to draw the strength he needed to continue.

The countryside has changed a great deal since that time and the sounds of human activity reach even the most remote parts of our small island. Traffic noise insinuates itself throughout much of the day and passenger jets add a deeper background rumble. Neither, however, is as intrusive as the roar of military planes or the sharp retort of sporting guns. Such abrupt sounds penetrate the calm in a manner that cannot be ignored.

It is only during the hours of night that a sense of stillness can truly be felt, as our activities dwindle though never quite cease altogether. It is then that the stillness descends, the evening song of robin and blackbird becoming more resonant, deepening the silence. The air feels heavier; you begin to pick out other natural sounds and feel more at one with your surroundings.

As individuals we benefit from the stillness of the natural world and the opportunity to settle within its embrace. It provides space for reflection, increases our sense of place and, importantly, is free from the sounds that would otherwise claw at our attention. We are so busy filtering out the artificial, day-to-day sounds of the world around us that we lose sight of the natural world and, by doing so, lose the all-important bond that helps to keep us rooted.

Plovers

The golden plover flock is anything but settled and it seems likely that they have been harassed by a peregrine or other raptor during recent days. Several hundred of these beautiful waders shuffle nervously on the exposed mud of one of the lagoons at Norfolk Wildlife Trust's Cley reserve. A multitude of gleaming black eyes alert to danger, it only needs one bird to take to the wing and the rest of the flock erupts with a clearly discernible rush of wings. The flock rises sharply, forming a coherent mass and taking on a life of its own, pulsing and twisting in the air, flicking from gold upperwings to a flash of white underparts. It is easy to see how a would-be predator might find it difficult to single out a victim. Moments later, the flock having circled, and birds begin to drop back down. Each time the flock goes up there are groans from the other end of the hide. A juvenile American golden plover was keeping company with this flock yesterday and some birdwatchers are keen to pick it out from its mass of slightly larger, warmer-coloured European relatives.

When you see the spectacle of a flock of waders on the wing, jinking and twisting through the air, it is easy to see their appeal. While some waders can be considered beautiful in their own right, the sight of many hundreds or thousands of individuals collected into a flock is truly amazing. They are not the only flock present today, with several hundred sleeping teal, a few dozen wigeon and a sizeable number of black-headed gulls, but they are the only spectacle. Every now and then the panic of the plovers triggers the gulls to take flight. But with the gulls there is no synchrony, no sense of individuals working together in unison. Instead, the gulls merely give a ragged show – a random flurry of white, lacking direction and purpose.

Flocking provides a number of benefits, including those related to predation risk. If you are part of a flock then your chances of being the target of a predator are reduced. Having others of your kind with you when feeding means that while you have your head down searching for food, another individual will almost certainly have its head up scanning for predators. Golden plover often flock with other birds, especially when they are feeding, and they can often be seen in the company of lapwing or black-headed gulls. While the smaller plovers may lose the odd piece of food to a larger gull, again there are the benefits of having more eyes to watch out for predators. And the benefit for us? A spectacular show.

Winter

A slither of snow held vertical
Cupped in a gentle loop of long dead hop.
Winter's window awaiting the breeze
that will see it fall once again.

A changing palette

It is early, although only if you judge the day by the time of its dawn. These short early December days give me longer in bed in the morning, the dogs stilled by the lingering dark outside, but soon after first light I am out in the forest.

In many ways these mornings are richer, the colour palette firmly based in deep hues and a raft of browns now that the dominant greens of summer have been sloughed. Although weakened, there is enough strength in the rising sun to draw out the tanned chestnut browns of the beech and soft yellows of the birch leaves that have clung so late this year.

On days when rain waits in close approach the sky is a deep Payne's grey. This dramatic backdrop frames the stand of beech, less than a dozen trees deep, that separates the forest block from the road beyond. The air is damp and holds within it the richly rounded scents of wood. The resinous smell of freshly cut pine hints at recent felling, a windblown giant cleared from the main track. At my feet, the rains from earlier in the week have rearranged the soil's surface. A dark, serpentine shape is revealed, as water finds the path of least resistance, carrying off the lightest grains of fine sand to expose the darker, more solid geology beneath.

Elsewhere in the forest, on the scruffy triangle of land where the willow warblers had their nest, the bracken has collapsed upon itself in a great seething mass. Its rough undulations give the appearance of a flooding torrent. Where the bracken has grown up through the scattered hawthorn it takes on a more dynamic form, appearing as waves breaking against the tangle of branches.

On the duller mornings the colour palette is much reduced, pared back to simple tones where soft brown and charcoal predominate. The landscape feels flat and, at times, almost two-dimensional. On other mornings, when dawn breaks following a clear night, frost tints the forest white. The once straw-brown stems of grass now glisten. Fallen branches, from which the bark has been lost, take on the appearance of polished bone. Curiously, the presence of a light frost seems to enhance the few patches of green that remain. Even the grand conifers have toned down their greens, the green of summer growth now hardened. It is a more brooding palette, one that suggests a land hunkered down and waiting. Come spring, the palette will change again.

House guest

I watch her some mornings as she moves across the wall; her eight stiletto-tipped legs find unseen purchase on the plaster, gravity-defying and assured in their hold on this world that exists in a vertical plane. Her body is just a few millimetres in length, darkly patterned and with an arc of tiny glistening eyes on the top of her head. I have not worked out which of our many spider species she is, in part because I do not wish to disturb her daily routine.

She is not alone, as other spiders lurk in the corners of this old house. Some are rarely seen and I suspect that they indulge in nocturnal scurryings long after we have turned in for the night. Others are chance encounters, seen briefly as they race across the carpet and dash under the sofa; big hairy beasts that spook our rather feeble hounds. Then there are the daddy-long-legs spiders that hang in untidy webs where wall meets ceiling. These fragile-looking spiders gyrate their bodies if disturbed, the motion so fast that the spider becomes little more than a pale blur, an effective and surprising defence for something so small.

Despite their ungainly appearance these daddy-long-legs spiders will tackle other spiders. Any that touch her web are approached and it is then that the long legs come into play. They give her greater reach, allowing silk drawn from the spinnerets to be flung over another spider with minimal risk. As well as other spiders, she will tackle small moths and mosquitoes, both unwelcome visitors to many homes. I sometimes spot the body of a white-shouldered house moth, partly wrapped in her silk.

One of the reasons why this house is so popular with these spiders is its age, meaning it lacks the dry warmth of modern houses, with their central heating and double-glazing. Like other house spiders, the daddy-long-legs spider can survive long periods without water but even she must descend to find it from time to time. Her eggs are thought to be prone to desiccation and presumably cannot cope in a modern house, with its dry heat.

I do not mind sharing our house in this way. Most of these other residents are innocuous enough and have little or no impact on our lives. The occasional visitor may go away with the impression that we are a little untidy, perhaps, but the scatter of webs and their delicate residents provides a sense of connection during these bleak winter months. We are sheltering together from the elements outside, a community of lives whose daily routines sometimes bring us into contact.

Horizons

As the fog concertinas the landscape so trusted horizons are lost and the countryside takes on a very different feel. With no sense of any real distance it is the closest hedgerows and trees that draw the eye, their bare limbs and branches stark against the flat sky, becoming two-dimensional in appearance. The ragged-winged forms of rooks materialise from the gloom and pass overhead like fragments of black cloth on an unfelt breeze. Sounds, too, are diminished, muffled by the fog, and I feel I am submerged within an unfamiliar landscape.

For some reason such days suggest a more ancient countryside, a land of wet fens and wild woods, and I half expect to see the dark shapes of lost tribes emerge from the fog; perhaps a shadowy band of Vikings, fresh from their victory over Edmund. It is a strange sensation but in some way it is also reassuring to feel some connection back through time with those who must also have passed over this land many centuries ago.

These damp days of early winter often bring with them a sense of melancholy that I find hard to shake. Perhaps it is the damp itself and the way in which its chill penetrates through layers of clothing to reach the bone within. More likely, it is the lack of the sun and its warming rays, rays that on a brighter winter's day would lift my mood. While I feel hemmed in by the shortened horizons, it does mean that I am forced to focus on my immediate surroundings, not tempted to let my gaze drift further afield.

In many ways I feel that I am experiencing my local patch anew; the familiar views have changed so much because of the fog that I almost lose my bearings. Certain trees gain in importance, appearing larger and more imposing now that they have been separated from their background. The fog also serves to shorten the day and it feels like late afternoon, even though it is not yet lunch.

Elsewhere, the blocks of plantation forest seem more threatening, their dark depths more foreboding and devoid of life. Even so, it is good to view this familiar part of my landscape in a way that is new, to feel uncertain about an area that I so often take for granted. While the presence of the fog has unsettled me, it has also forced me to look at things in a different way and sometimes this is a good thing.

An explosion of teal

The teal are nervous, occasionally spooking themselves into an explosion of wings for no obvious reason. There are well in excess of 300 of them here, gathered on this disused gravel pit in a loose extended flock. Most of the birds are towards the back of the pit, where the backdrop of reeds hints at shallower water; a smudge of grey forms on the darker pool. In with them are a few tufted duck, a single gadwall and a solitary male shoveler. It is reassuring to see them here in such numbers.

We are stood well back, shielded somewhat by more reeds. As we scan the flock – there is the outside chance of a vagrant green-winged teal from North America – it becomes apparent that the birds are unsettled. Groups of a dozen or so birds take to the wing in alarm and then splash down again, triggering others to respond in a similar fashion. The effect reminds me of a small child striking the surface of a puddle with a stick to generate splash after splash. Every now and then whole flock takes to the air, wheeling above us before dropping back onto the water.

Many of these teal will be winter visitors, arriving from Scandinavia, the Baltic States and western Siberia to join our largely resident breeding population. The numbers wintering within the UK are of international significance and many thousands may gather on the north Norfolk coast, around the Wash or across the Broads each winter. The flock before us is certainly one of the largest counts to have been made at this particular site, located deep within the Norfolk Brecks.

The teal is our smallest native duck and also one of the most attractive. Breeding plumage males sport a chestnut head, with deep green sides that are bordered with pale yellow. They are neat little birds, agile in flight and apt to form densely packed flocks. Small parties may be encountered on sheltered pools and quieter stretches of river, the birds readily flushed if disturbed. I usually only see teal in these numbers on the coastal grazing marshes so to have a flock of this size so close to home is a welcome sight.

Harrier

A familiar silhouette catches my eye as we drive down the muddy track that winds between the pools. 'Harrier' I call, but Dave doesn't quite catch the bird before it drops back below the treeline. He's not sure; it could be something else and we stop the car to check. The bird soon reappears, drifting towards us in the early morning light, its wings held in a shallow 'V'. It is a marsh harrier, long-winged and pale-headed, a young bird and one of only a handful of sightings from this inland site.

The presence of the harrier is an encouraging sign, reflecting a species whose population is increasing and whose breeding range is now expanding. There are now more breeding marsh harriers in England than at any other time during the last 200 years but their history has been a mixed one.

The marsh harrier seems to have been a familiar sight to the Norfolk naturalists writing in the mid-1800s. Lubbock, for example, writing in 1845, noted how every Norfolk pool of any extent had its pair, but numbers declined rapidly to leave just a single English pair at Horsey in 1911. The following decades saw a small recovery but it was not until the 1980s that the breeding population reached a size where the bird's future as a breeding species no longer looked precarious.

The return of the marsh harrier to East Anglia has been dramatic, the increasing number of breeding pairs year on year revealing a remarkable change in fortunes. East Anglia has become the stronghold for the species within Britain and it is the Broads and north Norfolk's coastal grazing marshes that support the greatest numbers. The harriers favour reedbed sites for nesting but have also taken to arable crops, such as wheat and oilseed rape, a preference that has opened up new opportunities for these birds within this largely arable landscape.

I suspect that there might not be a sufficiently large reedbed to attract breeding harriers to the site we work but it is just possible that a pair might give it a go. We know that they breed not far from here and if nothing else we expect to see more here over the coming years.

Frost

The brightness of the moon, descending towards dawn, leaves the clear-fell bathed in light. Dead grass stems, thickened with frost, have the appearance of fragile bone, creating an expanse of pale colour that contrasts with the dark depths of the silent conifers standing sentinel behind. Each of my two dogs leaves a visible cloud of exhaled air, like two furry steam trains puffing their way along the forest track. It is the end of a beautiful night and a bright clear morning lies ahead.

Overhead a procession of rooks is heading out from their overnight roost to seek food in the surrounding fields. The rooks are early risers, unlike the woodpigeons who stumble from sleep and their treetop perches as I approach the shelterbelt that runs alongside this part of the track.

A bird rises from the verge ahead of the dogs, a rounded body carried on broad wings – a woodcock and my first of the winter in the forest. They are not uncommon here at this time of the year, resting by day in the cover of the forest and feeding by night on the soft arable that surrounds it. Presumably, they must feed in the shadow of the forest on nights like this when the frost crisps the soil's surface and makes probing for worms that much more difficult within the open fields.

A larger shadow can be seen further ahead, slipping quietly across the track before pausing to take stock of me and the dogs. It is the fox whose scent I often smell along this particular stretch, stringent and clawing on the throat. Satisfied, it slips into the undergrowth and away. A late tawny owl calls, the call itself somewhat shrill and incomplete. Perhaps this is a young bird setting up territory for the first time. The call is sufficient, however, for one of the resident birds to respond with a mature, resonant hoot. Soon other birds respond, a brief overture of noise before silence returns.

It is then that I pick up the flight calls of redwing passing overhead. These birds may be on the move because of the colder conditions pushing in from further north. Frozen ground can spell disaster for them, restricting access to the soil-dwelling invertebrates on which they depend. These small thrushes seem to exist on a knife-edge at this time of the year, on the move continually to seek out the best feeding conditions and making journeys that may carry them south into continental Europe or west towards Ireland.

A Christmas tune

The dark gloom of these December mornings is softened somewhat by the wistful tunes of singing robins. While all our other songsters have fallen silent, the robin continues to sing in defence of its territory throughout the winter months. Holding a territory is incredibly important for a robin and it is only during the most severe of winter weather that the pattern of territories breaks down altogether. Even the females may set up their own winter territories, often close to where they will breed the following season, again proclaiming ownership through song. The winter song contains certain phrases that denote territory ownership and these also appear in the subtly different breeding season song. What are missing from the winter song though are the sexual phrases used in establishing a bond with a mate.

There is a strong tradition associating this confiding and popular bird with Christmas and it is always interesting to see how many Christmas cards arrive with a robin on their cover. In fact, robins first appeared on cards soon after the custom of sending cards at Christmas first took off commercially back in the 1860s. David Lack, writing in his famous book '*The Life of the Robin*', noted that the use of the robin on Christmas cards probably stemmed from similarity of the robin's red breast to the bright red uniform worn by Victorian postmen; many of the early card designs showed a robin with an envelope in its mouth.

Despite its confiding nature, and our enduring affection for this bird, it is worth noting that the robin can be a particularly quarrelsome species. The territorial song and red breast are important components of a display used to deter other robins from trespassing on an established territory. While the song proclaims 'this is mine, stay away', the red breast is used in more direct encounters. During a territorial dispute two robins will begin by singing at each other, with the territory owner attempting to sing from a higher perch than the intruder. This enables him to show off his red breast to maximum effect. If, for some reason, the territory holder finds himself positioned below the intruder he will throw his head back, again to maximise the amount of red breast on display. Such displays are usually sufficient to see off the intruder, but if not a ferocious fight may break out. The red breast is so important in this pattern of behaviours that a robin will even attack a bunch of red breast feathers. So, as the season of goodwill approaches – with the robin as its symbol – it is worth remembering that our beloved national bird has another side to its character.

New beginnings

New Year's Day is all about fresh beginnings, the old year gone and the new rich with opportunity. It is a day to be out in the countryside and to find the space and landscapes that afford quiet reflection. The weather is sometimes bright and crisp, at other times wet and windy, but almost always cold and invariably of a kind to clear away the end of year cobwebs and any signs of drowsiness that may come from the previous night's celebrations.

In some years I work my local patch but more commonly I head further afield, either west to the fenland margins or east to the valleys of the Waveney or the Yare. These landscapes bring with them big skies and distant horizons, providing a very different sense of scale that adds to the mood of reflection. Being out and active is invigorating; my new field notebook collects the first nature notes and bird sightings of the year.

In the past I have been known to participate in the occasional New Year's Day bird race, travelling around the county with friends to see just how many different bird species can be notched up in a day. Such events tend to be rather hectic affairs; while delivering a rush of adrenalin and the company of friends, they lack the opportunity to spend time taking in individual birds and the landscape within which they are placed.

Increasingly, I find that my greatest pleasure from birdwatching comes from spending time watching the birds in their habitat, studying their behaviours and following their interactions. This more engaged, often reflective form of birdwatching has come with a growing awareness of the natural world. No longer are the birds viewed as objects against a backdrop; instead, they have become part of that landscape – the background brought to the foreground and given equal prominence.

Today, I think I will head east once the sun is up, skirting the southern fringe of Norwich to access the marshes that border the river beyond Cantley. There is a good chance of some grey geese, good numbers of duck and, just possibly, bearded tit and peregrine. There is also the chance of spotting a Chinese water deer, a species best seen in this part of the county and northwards towards the Broads. I can already feel a rising sense of anticipation, of the joy of being out and about in the countryside on the first day of a new year.

Goldeneye

The ice changes everything; it shifts the focus away from familiar sites that I would normally search for wintering waterfowl. The lakes, so often packed with coot and duck, are empty. Instead they carry a crisp skin of newly formed ice, highly polished thanks to the lack of wind and reflecting the bank-side willows with photographic precision. The fishermen, quite sensibly, are nowhere to be seen and I have the reserve to myself.

Much of the activity is on the river which, ever in motion, remains ice-free. Small groups of mallard drift away at my approach, while the more nervous teal take flight, leaping into the air and away with a flurry of wings. Canada geese and feral greylags wander about the margins of the pits, unsure and seemingly bemused at the sudden change of state of their watery haunts. As they move across the shiny surface they slide each webbed foot forward, pushing down onto the ice. Am I imagining this or are they really indulging in something that resembles gentle skating? There is a sound to their somewhat unsteady movements, a harsh scratching noise, and I cannot work out if this is caused by their claws or comes from the ice itself, moving under the stresses of this additional weight. In some places the ice is thinner and the occasional goose falls through; with much flapping of wings it tries to move forward, the ice sometimes breaking further but more often the goose shaking itself free of the cold, dark water.

A larger area of open water holds a few dozen coot, a handful of tufted duck, a single goosander and, amazingly, a drake goldeneye. This stunning black and white duck is a rare visitor to the lakes, being more commonly encountered on the flooded margins of the East Anglian coast. Although there is a small but expanding breeding population in Scotland, this bird may have come from the larger Scandinavian population which breeds on freshwater lakes and pools surrounded by conifer forest. It is also remarkable that this particular bird is an adult male, since it is the females, which winter further south than the males, that dominate our wintering population.

Since the light is pretty good I get a decent chance to watch the goldeneye through my telescope as it dives deep into the lake in search of food, buoyantly erupting from the surface at the end of each dive. It won't remain here for long, especially if the ice increases its grip on the lake, so I am fortunate indeed to have stumbled across it.

Snowscape

Fresh snow transforms the landscape, bringing with it a shift in my mood, and I am quick to leave the house to walk favourite haunts under these new but temporary conditions. My first stop is the forest. Just as dawn breaks I christen its immaculate carpet of crisp white with the crunch of my footfalls. The dogs love the snow; it is an edible carpet that tickles their ever-inquisitive noses and they seem more playful than usual. The lines of dark conifers become part of an optical illusion. Last night's snowfall has coated their trunks with thin vertical brushstrokes of white, covering a narrow part of the darker trunks. In the half-light of dawn these lines of white become the trunks themselves, shrinking these great trees into mere spindles, now top-heavy with snow.

The snow reveals the passing of other creatures; deer, rabbits and even a fox have crossed my path overnight, animals whose presence would have otherwise gone unnoticed. Still, mine are the first human steps on these trackways and for now this landscape is mine.

Two hours later, and with the dogs now drying off at home in the kitchen, I am out again, down to the lakes to see if the cold weather has brought more ducks in from further east. Now that the day is properly awake, the brightness of the seamless blue sky and white landscape combine to produce a light that is more intense than that of mid-summer but less saturated with colour. Dark branches of the riverside alders stand silhouetted against the sky, each branch supporting a line of fresh snow. So still is the day that even the rambling, wire-like stems of the hops which grow wild here carry their own pinch of snow. One piece of stem, which loops about itself, supports nearly two inches of snow, a wafer-thin column that defies gravity.

Small flurries of snow fall from the treetops as a small party of siskins works its way ahead of me, feeding on the alder cones to the accompaniment of shrill but chatty calls. Larger showers of snow are dislodged by cumbersome woodpigeons that explode from their roosts, alarmed by my sudden arrival, and these drift down like a fine mist to settle cold on my face. Soon I am away from the river and out of the wood, skirting the lakes. I am no longer alone; two fishermen pace up and down near their rods to keep warm. Have they been here all night? I move further down the reserve, heading towards the quieter lakes where the wild ducks rest undisturbed. The stillness remains, punctuated only by duck calls and the crunch of footfalls on fresh snow.

Harbinger

The crows are ever-present companions on my walks these days. More often than not their presence is a silent one; a hunched form perched high in a bare tree or a ragged shadow slipping across the darkening winter sky. On such days, with brooding clouds and a bitter wind, it is easy to think of them as harbingers of an approaching storm and I can understand why crows and ravens have a central role in much of our folklore. Yet they so often remain bit-part players, a supporting cast to the more noticeable birds and animals with which I share my ramblings.

Throughout literature, the crow has nearly always been regarded as a sinister bird, a creature of ill omen. Perhaps some of this reputation was gained by the crow's association with death; as a scavenger it would have been present at the aftermath of great battles or quick to exploit the macabre offerings available at the many gibbets and gallows that once dotted our countryside.

Traits central to the success of various members of the crow family may also have lent weight to a belief in their having supernatural powers. Often long-lived, extremely bright and with a good memory, crows may exhibit behaviours that seem too advanced for 'mere birds'. Odin was held to have two ravens, named Hugin and Munin (Thought and Memory), who flew far and wide to bring him information. Anyone who has studied crows closely will know of their ability to retain information; such skills may have been revealed when crows were kept as pets.

Other powers have also been associated with various members of the crow family. The traditions of crow, raven and jay stones all associate some power with these birds, which is then held in a stone. Holding a crow stone conferred upon the bearer the gift of prophecy, while holding a jay or raven stone was believed to render you invisible. One aspect of crow folklore that has long interested me is the tradition of warriors or other people becoming crows. A local Cornish legend has it that King Arthur became a chough (or possibly a raven) after his death, while there is a French tradition that has wicked priests turned into ravens and bad nuns turned into crows!

While a modern day naturalist might laugh at such tales, they do provide an interesting insight into the degree to which we have now become divorced from the natural world, its creatures losing some of the power we once bestowed on them.

In search of gold

It is not yet dawn and the near silence of the forest echoes with the calls of a solitary crow, a sentinel for the slowly approaching day. We've arrived early, knowing that we have but a small window of opportunity to catch up with one of the golden pheasants that held territory in these forest blocks last year. It is still early in the season but, given the mild conditions and our need to pin down where the birds are, these weekend visits have become something of a ritual.

Despite its stunning plumage, the male golden pheasant is a rather challenging bird to catch up with. The species is not native to Britain but its small, self-sustaining population may be gaining importance in a global sense. The stronghold here is the dark stands of conifers that dominate the Norfolk/Suffolk borderlands of the Brecks. There is another, smaller, population in northwest Norfolk and other isolated records from elsewhere in Britain, typically of local escapees or recent introductions. These are rather secretive birds, spending most of their time within the cover provided by the stands of conifers and venturing out onto the rides for just a short period around dawn, hence our early visits.

Smaller than the common pheasant, whose vast numbers dominate much of the East Anglian landscape, the male golden pheasant has a stunning yellow head and crown, a red and blue body and a long and intricately patterned tail. One of his most striking features is the orange, black and blue feathering that adorns his neck. These feathers fall away from the body in the manner of a judge's wig, a wig in which the colour has been lifted from the finest casket of an Egyptian ruler, shrouded and laid to rest in a royal burial chamber.

This particular morning, like the last, we draw a blank in our search. The pheasants are here, of that we are confident, and one weekend soon we will be treated to an audience with his imperial majesty, the golden pheasant.

Swollen river

The river is a powerful force, especially now that it has
become swollen by last week's rain. For much of its length
the river gives the illusion of being inert; a soft brown,
gently flowing mass that moves down an imperceptible
gradient on a course that will, eventually, bring it to the
sea. It is only where the river is divided, with part of its
volume squeezed through a narrow weir, that its true
power is revealed in a roar of spray and noise.

This winter river is very different from that of late
summer and it is difficult to picture how it looked just
a few short months ago. It is brown rather than clear
and the lush growth of aquatic vegetation has long since
gone, rotted down and now part of the detritus held in
suspension like some full-bodied broth. The bank-side
willows are bare, their slim leaves now covering the banks.

While there is an air of decay about the river, the
riverside creatures bring a sense that spring will soon be
upon us and the river will once again return to life. On
bright days, early mistle thrush and great tit can be heard
singing, while great spotted woodpeckers indulge in
'chase-me' games high among the bare branches. The grey
wagtails are calling, their bouncy flight catching the eye
as they move up and down the stretch of water near the
weir. They have bred here in the past but in recent years

have favoured a different nest site further downstream. It seems that there are still sufficient insects along the river to sustain them through this difficult season. A pair of goosander hints that these sawbills might breed on the river again this year, a new and recent pattern that adds an exciting dimension to my riverside walks.

The other week there was an otter sighting a mile upstream; a cub just a few weeks old and the first confirmed breeding record for some years. It is another encouraging sign but, with the river rising by over a foot in recent days, there is concern for its safety; is it safe in a secure holt?

There is something remarkable about the river. Perhaps it is its changing moods, matching the seasons but also, in some small way, independent of them. The fact that on a bright summer day one part of the river can be shallow and babbling like the proverbial brook, while another, shaded by the willows, can be dark and sullen. Even in the depths of winter the river can be many things, always changing and ever my companion.

Squealer

The winter landscape feels open; last year's growth is now brittle beneath my feet and the chill of the wind cuts into my exposed flesh as sharply as the dry reeds that edge the narrow path. Summer's green and lush vitality, expressed through the aromatic growth of fenland plants, has been replaced by the crisp bleached browns of umbellifer stalks, now dead, and windblown branches. Other than the sound of the reeds being pushed against one another by the wind, there is little other noise. For a few brief minutes I am treated to the twittering calls of a tit flock as it moves through the alders in search of food but even these birds do not linger.

Then, quite suddenly, I hear it: an abrupt whistling squeal reveals the presence of a water rail. It is close by, ahead of me in the reeds but hidden from view. This retiring bird, with its repertoire of grunts, squeaks and squeals, is one of the real characters of the bird world. Seen well, it is possible to appreciate the mix of colours that adorn this clown of the fens. The rich brown back, streaked with black, and the soft grey of the neck and breast may seem plain enough but the zebra-striped flanks, red eye and red, slightly down-curved, bill add a sense of showmanship. Still, this is a reclusive clown and is more often seen, if seen at all, disappearing into the reeds with a flash of its undertail coverts and a smooth swift gait. This gait has given rise to the local name 'skitty cock' in some parts of England – the word 'skit' originally meaning to move lightly and rapidly – but it is the water rail's calls that give rise to a more lasting name, one that has its origins in Norfolk. During the 1800s, when water rails and their eggs appeared regularly on the stalls of Norwich market between March and May, it was known as a 'sharmer'. Since then, this name has been adapted to refer to the piercing calls uttered by the rail, reminiscent of squealing piglets, and known widely as 'sharming'. It is this name that appears in the textbooks.

During the winter months, when continental immigrants join our resident birds, you stand your best chance of seeing a water rail. If temperatures fall below zero, freezing over favoured waterbodies, then water rails may be forced from cover in search of food. At such times they may also supplement their largely insectivorous diet with carrion or fresh meat, the latter sometimes taken in the form of small birds stabbed or grabbed and drowned. This is a clown with a sinister side.

Rook

There is no denying that the fenland landscape can be bleak, dominated as it is by vast skies and with little to break the spirit-level flat horizon. Dull winter days bring brooding skies, the colour leaching from the land and only the deep peaty darkness of the rich black soils remaining. The wildlife often seems pushed to the margins here and the intrusive sounds of farm machinery and overhead aircraft remind you that this is a landscape in servitude to our own needs and whims.

At the same time, there are moments when the Fens can deliver great beauty and, sometimes, a sense of remoteness and closeness to nature. The other morning, for instance, I found myself at Ely station, waiting for a connection into Cambridge. It was still early and a broad sweep of horizon was blushed with soft purples and reds, a legacy of the changing weather and a weak winter sunrise. The sky, deeply patterned, was stunningly beautiful, with a real sense of depth. The feeling of great distance, a sense often felt in these flat lands, was further deepened by the stark silhouettes of distant poplars, two fields away. Few of my fellow passengers seemed to notice the breaking dawn, suffused with colour. Perhaps they were too engrossed in their phones, papers or morning coffee to notice the spectacle of this fenland morning.

Above the murmurings of chattering people could be heard the more strident calls of rooks, a steady but loose stream of birds crossing the sky and most likely freshly emerged from a communal overnight roost. The calls of these birds, less harsh in tone than those of the equally familiar carrion crow, speak of these fenland landscapes. These early nesters hint at the first stirrings of spring, of what is to come with the passing of a few more weeks and with the strengthening of the sun.

The colour of the sky soon changes and the beauty slips away as the colour slides from purple into grey. Then the moment is gone. My train arrives and I manage to grab a window seat to watch the landscape roll past me: dark soils, narrow ditches and fields that appear as vast lakes, so well are they covered in warming polythene. A small group of whooper swans loafing in a field, a flight of wild ducks and a thick-coated roe buck all slip by. There are days when I love the Fens and others when I struggle to find any attachment, so bleak do they seem. There is always some emotional response to this great landscape.

Winter walk

The wind has dropped but clear skies overnight mean that the air carries a sharp chill and my breath clouds as I exhale. It is a fine day for a walk; the quality of the light, filtered through a brilliant blue sky, reveals every fold in the landscape and the bare limbs and branches of trees stand strong in silhouette. Crossing fields of grazed pasture, bordered by old hedgerows and occasional twisted oaks, my passing is heralded by a pair of Egyptian geese – soon to be nesting in a suitably large cavity. A flock of fieldfares, perhaps three dozen strong, chatters quietly as it moves across the short turf in search of invertebrate prey. There has been just the merest touch of frost, the fieldfares still able to probe the ground.

Leaving the farmland, I enter an area of clear-fell. Now in their second year of growth, the young conifers can be seen fighting their way up through the early successional plants that are quick to exploit the bare soil. As I cross diagonally through the regimented lines I disturb a roe deer – a buck in his thick winter coat. He moves away but then turns to watch me, inquisitive but alert. This seems to be a feature of the roe. This buck is in velvet, his antlers sheathed in blood-rich tissue which will remain in place through into March. In adult males this annual cycle of renewal begins late in the year (from

October) but starts somewhat later in young bucks. With his curiosity satisfied the roe moves off and I am alone again, save for the solitary crow calling from an isolated beech.

A little further on, and warmed by my exertions and the strengthening sun, I catch sight of a kestrel. It passes low over the trees in a neighbouring block of plantation before dipping down to work one of the snag lines of twisted root plates left in place when the last block of timber was harvested. The kestrel flushes a flock of goldfinches but seems to take no interest in them. The goldfinches rise as one to perch in a nearby birch, their delicate calls resonant like tiny chimes.

It may be winter but it is a fine and bright winter, with enough of the sun's warmth creeping through to suggest that spring is not that far away.

Roost

It will not be long until dusk. The muddy footpath makes progress difficult and lodges in my mind the unsettling suspicion that we will arrive too late and so miss the promised spectacle. We've come to Lakenheath Fen, one of our regular haunts, in order to see the growing roost of marsh and hen harriers that has been something of a feature this winter. Although the marsh harriers can be seen here throughout the day, and indeed throughout the year, the hen harriers are a seasonal visitor, arriving on the short winter afternoons shortly before dusk.

The walk out yields up two barn owls and a Slavonian grebe, the latter rare inland and the first I have seen in the Brecks. A herd of mute swans, 32 in number and feeding in a pasture, hints at the visiting whooper and Bewick's wintering further out into the fens, but our journey today ends here, a small group of us stood on the banked footpath and looking back across the reserve. Off to our left is a larger group of birdwatchers, dutifully gathered at the crane watchpoint, but ours is the better position, shaped by local knowledge and the position of the low winter sun.

Within moments we have our first harriers, two marsh and a single male hen harrier. He is a stunning male, the grey wings readily picked out against the dark of the marsh and the line of trees and shrubs beyond. Soon we pick out others, our counts reaching at least five different individuals. As well as the harriers, there are a perched peregrine, the resident pair of cranes and a passing kestrel. As the light begins to go, so two of the hen harriers continue to hunt, coming closer and closer to where we are standing. The views are breathtaking as the harriers float by on owl-like wings, occasionally checking their buoyant flight to hover over possible prey.

The roost this year is almost certainly the best it has ever been, surpassing the numbers being seen elsewhere within the region and providing a good number of visiting birdwatchers with a fantastic late winter spectacle. This spectacle includes not just the birds but also the fenland landscape and the dramatic late winter sky.

After the storm

It is good to be able to slip from the house at dawn and to enter a world that is finally still. The biting and bracing wind has passed and the air holds the carrying notes of song thrush and woodpigeon, both of which hint at the approaching spring. February is a dark month; part of winter's realm, she carries not the new year hope of January but instead sits belligerent and brooding. A troublesome month of storms, of rain and rising waters, of a wind that never drops. Will spring ever come?

These final days of the month, however, give hope, and the calm that greets this dawn suggests a season soon to change. While I have seen these false hopes before, the hints of spring snuffed out by a weather system bringing chill winds from the north or squally rain from the west, the blooms of snowdrop, aconite and winter heliotrope offer a glimpse of the season to come.

And there, among the brash that needs clearing from around the pond, I find a female brimstone. Her yellow-green sulphur colour proclaims life amid the blacks and dirty browns of rotting wood and leaf. Tenderly, I take her folded wings between thumb and forefinger and place her within the green ivy that coats the ancient wall. She will be safe and sheltered here, ready to stir with the first run of truly warm days.

The small tortoiseshells wintering in our unheated upstairs toilet have already shown their restlessness. On warmer mornings, when the sun's rays push in through the small window, these wintering house guests can be found fluttering around the upstairs of the house. Come evening, when they are perched on curtain or net, I return them to 'their' room.

Droppings in the side passage, both on the flagstones and stuck to the wall, reveal that the brown long-eared bat has also been active. There are few moths coming to the lighted windows at night, so he may be better off remaining in whichever cavity he has chosen for the winter. Perhaps, as it is with me, these stirrings are a response to the changing weather, the lengthening of the days and the turning of the season.

New tenants

The spoil heaps outside the old fox earth have grown in size over recent weeks, a sure sign that new tenants are in place. The loose sandy-coloured soil spills from these heaps down the steep leaf-strewn slope and into the dark waters that sit silently below. It is an odd location, positioned as it is at the top of a crumbling slope that eats its way into a small block of woodland. Well-worn paths lead away from the five different entrances, along the very top of the slope and into the wood itself. Not wanting to approach too closely, I can only scan the compacted soil of the entrances with my binoculars, but this fails to reveal a clear footprint that would identify what creature has taken ownership.

The entrances themselves have been enlarged quite considerably and the weak winter sunlight shining directly into one of these is sufficiently strong to reveal that the tunnel remains wide even as it disappears underground. Could it be that badgers have taken ownership? There have been occasional sightings from nearby over recent years, so perhaps this is a sign of a resurgent badger population, expanding into new areas. Norfolk does not hold the number of badgers seen in more southerly or westerly counties.

Badgers prefer loose, free-draining soils and need to be near arable land or grassland where they can forage for food. Many areas within the county are too low-lying but some parts are both suitable and well used. This particular spot is relatively free from disturbance so may have proved attractive to the badgers. Our understanding of Norfolk's badgers is improving, mainly due to the efforts of interested volunteers who have championed these wonderful animals, spending many hours searching for and documenting active setts.

A quick search through the wood, following the obvious paths that radiate out from the potential sett, reveals evidence that bedding has been dragged towards the entrances, but there is no sign of the shallow pits containing badger faeces, known as badger latrines, that I would expect to see. Since these have a social and territorial function it may be the wrong time of year to come across them. Although badgers do not undertake a true hibernation, they do reduce the levels of activity during the winter months. This suggests that I will need to return in spring in order to find out if it really is badgers who have taken up residence.

Songsters

There have been a few warmer days of late, premature hints of a spring that is still a number of weeks away. Such teasing glimpses make February burdensome – winter can't still be upon us? I want to get out and watch nature springing into life. I am not the only one eager to get going, for outside in the early morning darkness a song thrush is singing, its strident notes striking out above the plaintive winter song of a robin.

The impression ones gets when listening to a song thrush is of a singer that enjoys the act of performance, something that is reflected in the bold clarity of the delivered phrases and the deceptive simplicity of structure. Each song thrush will have a repertoire of a hundred or more different phrases and appears to select from these almost at random, putting several together and often repeating a sequence a number of times over.

This fondness for a rhythmic repetition of repeated phrases may be one of the reasons why the song thrush features so prominently in poetry. One of the best examples of this comes in Tennyson's '*The Throstle*' but others, including Thomas Hardy, Robert Browning and Edward Thomas, all draw on this English songster. Edward Thomas, undoubtedly the least well known of these poets, featured our various thrushes in 15 or so of his 142 poems and his use of colloquial speech rhythms is well suited to the repetitive nature of the bird's song.

The presence of repeated phrases, so characteristic of the song thrush, proves very useful for separating this species from another late winter songster, the mistle thrush. The latter species has a song that is more reminiscent of a blackbird, though harsher in tone and with a faster tempo. This is delivered from the upper branches of a tree and is loud and far-carrying.

Many authors have commented upon the feeling of sadness that derives from the mistle thrush's song. Perhaps this is added to by its habit of singing on bleak, overcast days or during periods of wind and rain, a behaviour that has earned it the local name of 'stormcock'. Although I admire the mistle thrush for singing, indifferent to the harsh backdrop of a late winter storm, I prefer the optimism offered by the song thrush: '*Spring is coming, spring is coming, spring is coming.*'

A wet walk

I have been marking time. Brooding over the weather, the wind and rain confining me to the house, I have been studying maps and planning which parts of the county to explore in the warmer, more welcoming days of spring and summer. Deciding that this won't do, that the weather will not restrain my wanderings, I dig out a thick woollen hat and my waterproof and head out.

With so much water in the air and seemingly oozing from the sodden ground I am drawn towards the river. The waters are brown with silt washed from the fields; in places they push their way up towards the lip of the bank, as if straining to reclaim the vast puddles that cover the bank-side path. The thin, elongated, fallen leaves of willow carpet the ground. Sodden with the rain, their grey undersides resemble small, lifeless fish, disgorged by the angry waters.

For a brief distance the path leads me away from the river, skirting a field and a small piece of alder carr, and here I encounter a muntjac. This one is a female; squat in shape and hunched against the elements it is uncertain at my approach, moving off slightly before turning to stare at me intently. Its thick coat must provide a good degree of protection from the rain. Finally, a decision is made and the small deer turns and is soon lost from view amongst the dripping vegetation. There is a real sense of decay in this wood; the fallen leaves and timber, last year's growth that has died back, are all brown and sodden. Only the leaves of the bramble stand out, green and vibrant and screaming of life.

By now the rain has eased somewhat, enough to bring out smaller birds intent on feeding before the light fades. Amid the many blackbirds is a song thrush, its warm tones welcome and lifting my spirits further. Then, as if seeing the song thrush was a good omen, I catch sight of a finch in flight. It is heavy and rounded in shape, and I follow its course, bringing my binoculars up to catch it land in one of the tall alders that flank the fen. It is a hawfinch, the first I have seen on my local patch and I feel unadulterated joy. I've seen these birds before, most winters in fact, at well-known local sites but this one is mine, on my patch and unexpected. Is this reward offered to me as an enticement – look at what you may see if you venture out – or is it pure chance that I stumbled across it? Either way, it is a wonderful bird to see at any time of year, no matter what the weather.

FEBRUARY

Index